I WANT TO BELIEVE

AN INVESTIGATORS' ARCHIVE

JASON HEWLETT

PETER RENN

BEYOND THE FRAY

Publishing

ISBN 13: 978-1-954528-17-8

Beyond The Fray Publishing, a division of Beyond The Fray, LLC, San
Diego, CA
www.beyondthefraypublishing.com

BEYOND THE FRAY

Publishing

CONTENTS

A FEW WORDS FROM PETER RENN

Over the years I have met many people from different realms of paranormal investigations who are all unique, and each hold credibility in the field. Each one has a different story on how he or she got into the profession, and have experiences that have kept them continually chasing their passion.

I am honored to be one of their peers, and even more honored that these people are my friends.

I hope you enjoy their stories and experiences. This is the foundation on why we do what we do.

1 CIARAN O'KEEFFE

As a pioneer in the paranormal investigative field, and one of the few who can be close to being called an expert, Ciaran O'Keefe jokingly refers to himself as two people.

The first is a serious parapsychologist who is also an applied psychologist and investigative psychologist, who also works in music psychology. He's an associate professor of education at Buckinghamshire University in the United Kingdom. This O'Keeffe is a serious and educated man who approaches the field of paranormal research with a skeptical mind and an eye for detail, with the education to back it up.

"As a parapsychologist, I'm involved in the scientific study of the paranormal, which I've been doing for about thirty years now," says O'Keeffe.

Then there's his Evil Twin Brother, who's been on a host of paranormal reality shows and documentaries like England's popular television series *Most Haunted*, *Jane Goldman Investigates*, *Ghost Adventures* and more.

"Being a parapsychologist, that's my scientific hat, and I publish and do research on that. I have another hat, ghost busting essentially, or ghost hunting... and I've been doing that for many, many years."

It was O'Keeffe's serious work in the field that attracted media attention, which he says came about naturally as his experience – and no-nonsense approach – became more and more noticed. To hear him talk about it, he's taken the notoriety in stride.

What sparked this career-making fascination with the paranormal? Most people who dedicate their life to this work can trace the interest back to a childhood experience, often an unexplainable and frightening encounter. Not so for O'Keeffe.

Instead, he grew up fascinated by ghost and horror stories. When he was eight and nine years old, he was reading Stephen King, H. P. Lovecraft, James Herbert and other genre staples. He read so much his parents actually became concerned, he says. As he hit his teens, shows like

Arthur C. Clarke's Mysterious World came along and fueled the interest even further.

In fact, he still has the full set of *Unexplained Magazine*, which he collected religiously as a boy.

The turning point for O'Keeffe came in 1984, when *Ghostbusters* stormed theatres and became a blockbuster hit. He says he contacted Columbia University and asked to join the parapsychology unit they had there. The secretary who answered the phone rebuked him, saying it was just a movie. In the end, he attended the Institute of Parapsychology in North Carolina.

That was what got O'Keeffe into the scientific side of the profession. His interest in the ghost-hunting side – the "flashier" side for lack of a better word - began with a walk on a beach when he was a teenager.

He was on vacation in the harbor village of Clovelly, in the district of Devon, and walking with his parents on the beach. As they walked, they passed a cave along the coast, and he felt a horrible chill.

"I didn't like the chill, as well as recognizing it was just really cold," he says.

The family finished their walk and returned to the village, stopping at the tourism information centre. On a table was a newspaper, opened to a fold-out story about how, some three hundred years earlier, there had been a cannibalistic family holed up in a cave on the coast, and this family was believed responsible for enough deaths in the area the population had dwindled considerably during the course of fifty or sixty years.

O'Keeffe put two and two together, in a way he admits could have been erroneous. He'd read the story and passed a cave that gave him a chill. In his mind, that was evidence he had walked by the cave where the cannibal family once lived.

"My experience then wasn't that this could be paranormal," he says. "My experience was, this could be something weird, but it could also be not the right cave. I'm feeling a chill now and reinterpreting it, or it could've just been cold down on the coast. There's any number of different reasons behind it."

He says there's something about his mind, partly fueled by his reading material at the time, that had him thinking rationally about that experience.

Another turning point for O'Keeffe came when he was sixteen or seventeen. He went ghost hunting at the mausoleum by Hellfire Caves in West Wickham and found himself in the undergrowth, armed with a night-vision scope. He spent all night lying in the grass, waiting for something to happen, and nothing ever did.

"Apart from a badger walked up next to me, about two feet away," he says.

This is not uncommon for a paranormal investigation, badger aside.

Looking back, O'Keeffe remembers the excitement of anticipation, the waiting for something to happen, playing over all the horror stories he'd read as a boy, and wondering if any of them could come true. He says that feeling was more important than the fact he didn't find anything. And it's what continues to fuel his interest and passion for the profession.

"It's like, what if?" he says.

O'Keeffe's approach to the field makes it difficult for him to highlight one personal experience that stands out over all the others. He's been on thousands of investigations, he says. And of those, there's about a hundred and fifty that other people would say are paranormal. These include sensing a presence he couldn't see, or even seeing something at the end of a hallway that perhaps was a spirit.

But O'Keeffe understands how environment and psychology come into play. He says this is a potential strength, as he can see the alternative explanation for what he and others are experiencing. It's also a potential weakness, as his rational mind immediately interprets what's going on into a rational explanation.

He's still able to view these experiences as being phenomenal and having the potential for there to be something paranormal going on. But he's able to see the psychological explanations as well. This he explains by providing some examples of personal experiences he's been a part of.

One such case involved an abandoned nightclub in Birkenhead, which is across the river from Liverpool, says O'Keeffe. Staff at the club decided to conduct a séance before the establishment closed down. Paranormal activity began after the séance, with fire doors opening on their own, shadows appearing and moving about where there shouldn't be any, and people sensing an unseen presence.

A team was invited to investigate, and spent six months conducting weekly investigations at the location. After about four months, O'Keeffe was brought in to help, and he experienced something toward the end of his time there.

He says the original staff members ended up at the club on the same night, which was purely accidental. A couple of them had asked to join that night's investigation, while the others happened to pass by, saw the lights were on, and asked to be a part of things when they found out what was going on.

"They suggested doing a séance exactly the same way they did that first night that kicked everything off," says O'Keeffe.

O'Keeffe admits he was hesitant, as he had no control over the impact such an experiment could have on people once they left the location. But he offered to counsel anyone on the off chance they had unexplainable experiences afterward. In the end, the decision was made to recreate the séance, using the exact same table, and having everyone sit in the same positions they had the first time.

"Which is an investigator's dream for them to do that," he says.

Armed with a thermal imager – which O'Keeffe always sets to black and white rather than color, as black and white shows a drop in temperature as green, making any shift easier to see – he asked the group to proceed with the séance. He filmed the entire event, and after about twenty or thirty minutes, the group wanted to stop, as nothing was happening.

O'Keeffe encouraged them to carry on, as this was a unique opportunity to investigate. If nothing happened after ten more minutes, they could call it a night.

What he didn't tell them was, out of the corners of the room, a green fog had started to form at ground level and move toward the table they were sitting at, he said. This green fog signaled a drop in temperature that was moving from the outside of the room in.

"As it started to get toward the table, a couple of people around the table said, 'It feels like the energy's building, it feels like something is happening'," he says. "And then they did some glass work on the table, which I'm cynical about, but they felt like it was really active in the messages they were getting."

This lasted about thirty minutes; then one of them said it felt like the energy was leaving. As she said that, the fog, which had hung around the table the entire time, began to dissipate, says O'Keeffe.

The team had USB monitors measuring temperature and humidity set up at key points around the location, especially doors and windows where disturbances were most likely to be detected. O'Keeffe says none of them picked up a drop in temperature when the green fog was detected on his thermal camera.

He says this was a fascinating encounter, as it had the subjective experience of those sitting around the table, who were interpreting the drop in temperature as some kind of paranormal energy building. Plus there was the thermal imager measuring a drop in temperature.

"That for me is a particularly weird experience, and I'd put it up there as one of my top experiences, which I still call a head-scratching moment. It's fleeting and it's gone.

There's no way of creating that again, as the nightclub is gone," says O'Keeffe.

It also shows how people's minds are primed to interpret data a certain way, he says. People have a strange experience somewhere in a place they've heard is haunted. Their brains are already set to expect anything that goes on there as possibly being paranormal.

Nor is a drop in temperature, which many associate with the appearance of a spirit, as accurate a gauge of paranormal activity as people think, says O'Keeffe.

"It could be purely psychological. It could be the adrenalin and fear kicking in, and feeling like a drop in temperature, when in fact there isn't," he says. "Similarly, it could be a draft. There could be quite a few explanations."

A drop in temperature is consistent with haunting phenomenon for as far back as people have been reporting them. O'Keeffe says not every alleged haunting comes complete with a drop in temperature, but the recordings are frequent enough to note. And, in modern ghost hunting, such a phenomenon can be recorded using the tools of the trade.

"It's there historically as far back as the ancient Greeks," he says, adding he'd like to see more research done on temperature and then shared among paranormal investigators.

In contemporary North America, EMF is the current fascination for paranormal investigators. A change in EMF, or the electromagnetic field, is believed to be a sign of a ghostly or spiritual presence. The problem is there could be a thousand and one factors as to why a room's electromagnetic field has been disrupted, including someone turning on a nearby microwave, a taxi driving by outside, or a text sent via cellphone.

The danger is people associate the flashing lights of an EMF detector with science, when it's not, says O'Keeffe. And an electromagnetic field, and even the Earth's geomagnetic field, can affect a person's brain, creating hallucinations and other experiences that are in line with paranormal phenomenon.

If investigators want to use a K2 meter, or other EMF or GMF detector, they should use it in a way that illustrates how the magnetic fields are impacting people's health during the alleged haunting, he says.

Looking back at past episodes of *Most Haunted*, there are times when host Yvette Fielding is shocked by O'Keeffe placing a K2 meter at a medium's head when she claims to feel a spirit's presence.

"Potentially, what I'm looking at is if the field is affecting them in some way," he says.

Even this is pseudoscience, says O'Keeffe. Ideally, one would triangulate the EMF's location using multiple detectors in multiple locations. In the end, using devices like this makes you look scientific, but it's an illusion.

"It's not used scientifically, the way it should be," he says.

So what does O'Keeffe use to investigate alleged hauntings? As a parapsychologist, he sticks with environmental monitoring equipment to measure humidity, air pressure, and light intensity. He will look for EMF, but focus more on measuring electric fields to gauge the influence they have on people's health. O'Keeffe also explores infrasound, or low-frequency sound, to see how it influences what the alleged haunted are thinking or feeling.

Infrasound waves are below levels the human ear can hear, but they can cause disorientation, nausea, anxiety and panic – many sensations that accompany reports of paranormal activity.

The ghost hunter in him always brings a thermal imager to a location, not only to track changes in temperature, but also because it allows him to see in the dark, in a situation where people don't know he can see in the dark.

"If you have a night-vision camera, people know that. But a thermal imager, people will very quickly forget you're able to see in the dark. And you'll be able to see if people throw something, and you'll also be able to see if someone pushes a table, or if somebody is around a corner," says O'Keeffe.

The key piece of equipment any ghost hunter should bring with them is something to record with, be it a camera, mobile phone, digital recorder or paper and pen, he says. Documenting what happens is the most important thing an investigator can do.

No matter what hat O'Keeffe wears, be it the scientist or the ghost hunter, the skeptic or the believer, he continues to maintain the same sense of "what if" he had lying in wait in the grass at Hellfire Caves when he was a teenager. Because even though the science can add up to a natural explanation for all he has seen and heard, in the end, we still don't know for sure.

2 PAUL BRADFORD

One of the first questions asked of anyone in the paranormal field is what got him or her interested in the subject
in the first place. Most of the time, it's something that
happened in the investigator's youth, often a close
encounter with something unexplained and, at the time,
quite frightening.

In Paul Bradford's case, it was too much television.

This shouldn't surprise anyone who knows Bradford, given he ended up hunting ghosts on television as a part of the popular *Ghost Hunters International*, which broadcast for three seasons on SyFy. He's recently appeared on the Travel Channel series *Trending Fear*.

But long before he was on television, Bradford was immersed in the world of science fiction and horror, both on the tube and silver screen. A self-professed nerd, he grew up a fan of pretty much anything with aliens in it, particularly *The X-Files*.

"Basically anything science fiction. I was all over it," he says.

Bradford was five when he saw the original *Ghostbusters*, and that was the first time he had the inkling it would be cool to hunt ghosts, he says. Flash forward to the mid 2000s, and he found himself an investigator with Sonora Paranormal Investigations in Arizona.

"It was just an interest for me. It wasn't like I'd had any profound experience or anything like that. It was purely an interest," says Bradford. "And really sort of a fascination to discover. Explore strange new worlds and all that."

Bradford fell into investigating strictly by happenstance. He'd moved to the United States from England and had applied for a work visa. He was unemployed and wanted something to pass the time. Given he was living in Arizona, where it's always hot, a daytime activity was out of the question, but his brother-in-law was part of Sonora Paranormal, and they were active at night.

"I just wanted to see what it was all about," he says of his first foray into ghost hunting.

Not long after joining Sonoran Paranormal, it became clear to Bradford there was little in the way of equipment available to paranormal investigators. There were no night-vision cameras and EMF meters. In fact, Bradford recalls only one consumer available camcorder that shot in night vision, and even then the scope of what could be recorded was limited to about seven feet.

As Bradford puts it, he was an adult with adult money more or less at his disposal, so he decided to build equipment for the team. His first invention was an IR light extender, which increases the field of vison for night-vision cameras to fifty feet. It's no surprise the invention took off, and it wasn't long before other teams asked Bradford to build lights for them.

Bradford spent a lot of time researching different equipment concepts, many of which were sold through GhostStop, an online equipment retailer for paranormal investigators. Browse the site, and there's a plethora of EVP recorders, cameras, lights, lasers and Spirit Boxes.

"Again, my nerdiness and love of sci-fi really came out in that," he says. "I started building a number of paranormal tools, which progressed over the years and got better over the years."

His IR light extenders are still used today, a good decade after he invented them, by teams all around the world.

"And I know there's one floating off the coast of Costa Rica, because we dropped it in the water," he says, recounting a *Ghost Hunters International* adventure.

Bradford is indeed one of the early paranormal television celebrities. *Ghost Hunters International* was a spin-off of *Ghost Hunters*, which launched in 2004 and broadcast for eleven initial seasons. Arguably the first paranormal reality show, *Ghost Hunters* followed the exploits of Jason Hawes and Grant Wilson of the Atlantic Paranormal Society.

Where *Ghost Hunters* covered haunted locations in the United States, *Ghost Hunters International* travelled around the world and documented some of the most legendary haunted locations. He was the technology manager alongside lead investigators Barry Fitzgerald, Kris Williams, Joe Chin, and Scott Tepperman. Susan Slaughter was the case manager.

How did Bradford get involved? Even after all these years, he appears slightly surprised by how it all came about.

"It stemmed from me building stuff. So basically I built stuff for my team and did investigations with other teams," he says, adding those teams asked him to build equipment for them. "And then I had people wanting to talk to me about the equipment that I was building, so I did a couple of interviews and things."

Out of the blue, one of the websites he'd been interviewed by contacted him, saying the team from *Ghost Hunters* were looking for him.

"My first thought was 'Oh shit, what did I do'," says Bradford.

There was an initial conversation via telephone followed by a formal interview, he says. Then he was asked if he wanted to join the *Ghost Hunters International* team.

Bradford's screen test involved a flight to Chile, where an episode was filming.

"It was a sink-or-swim moment. Fortunately, I didn't sink too much," he says.

Given all the investigations he's done, one would think it would be tough to pick one experience or case that stands out from the rest, especially given the television angle. But Bradford quickly lists the Quarantine Station in Manly, Australia, as a personal favourite. He admits it came about strictly as a desire to prove he belonged on *Ghost Hunters International*.

Originally known as North Head Quarantine Station, the site was used from the 1830s to 1984 to isolate people who were migrating to Australia and suspected of carrying infectious diseases. The station is now considered a heritage site and is home to a hotel, conference centre, and restaurant complex.

It's also considered one of the most haunted locations in Australia and has been home to ghost tours since the 1990s.

Bradford decided he wanted to head off and investigate on his own, so he opted to go into the old morgue, which is still a part of the historic structure at the station. He says it was just himself and a mounted camera, no one else.

In order to "get into the right mindset", he lay down on an old slab where the corpses were laid out. What happened during the course of his investigation, he'll never forget. Bradford says he heard footsteps inside and outside the room and movement going on all around him.

The effort paid off, as he received a phone call from an executive at SyFy a month later, before the episode was broadcast.

"They were like 'That's how you do a solo investigation'," he says. "For me, it was just awesome because I was reacting to everything as far as I'd hear something, and then go and investigate."

Too many paranormal shows will depict investigators hearing something, acknowledging it, and then not following up with an investigation, says Bradford. He sees every bit of activity as a way to tell a story with a beginning, middle and end.

"You hear a noise, and you think it's a car or you think it's something, but go and investigate. Go see what it is. Create that story. If it gets to the end and it's a car, yeah, great. But you validated it," says Bradford.

"It works both ways. You say, 'Yeah, it's a car.' But there are no cars. 'That's just somebody coming up the stairs.' But there is no one coming up the stairs. It validates what you've heard."

While the Quarantine Station provided the best paranormal experience, it was an exploration of the Mayan underground in Belize that is Bradford's favourite personal experience. The *Ghost Hunters International* cast and crew trekked along river systems and through forests and ventured miles underground into a vast cave system.

Everyone had to wade through underground rivers, scramble up rocks, and climb waterfalls to get to the end of the caves, he says. When the team got there, they climbed into this vast cathedral where there was pottery and evidence of past sacrifices to the Mayan gods.

"You could see the [cave] started with grain, then there'd be animal bones and, at the end, there was actually fossilized remains of a Mayan princess. Quartz had actually grown over the bone, so it preserved it," says Bradford.

"They actually referred to it as the Crystal Maiden. It was fascinating. It was really, really fascinating."

Like many boys, Bradford wanted to be James Bond or Indiana Jones when he grew up. He says the Belize adventure was his way of being Indiana Jones, if only for a short while. The paranormal investigator experience is as close as anyone can get to searching for the Lost Ark.

"I was Indiana Jones."

Not everyone who becomes a paranormal investigator has the chance to star in a reality television series. In fact, the odds of that happening are rare. So Bradford has had the rare opportunity to have investigated in front of the camera.

Within the paranormal community, there is a stigma associated with television investigators, one that is largely driven by reports of teams faking evidence and staging scares in the name of driving up ratings. Indeed, there is a lot of pressure on cast and crew to deliver the goods and please producers and networks.

When it comes to filming for television, the investigation itself isn't that different compared to investigating as a team with no crew following you around, says Bradford. The camera and sound department were there to document what the team was doing, and largely stood back and let the investigators do their thing.

Once the investigation is done, all the "TV stuff" comes into play, he says. Evidence reveals, interviews, and site tours take place. This often requires multiple camera set-ups and shooting different scenes over and over again according to the demands of the director, producer, and network.

"When it came to the investigation part, we ran it," says Bradford.

He likens the experience to filming a documentary, where camera teams film everything and then the story is built afterwards. In Bradford's mind, that's the whole point of reality television.

Bradford has heard of cases where the pressures to stage and fake things have occurred on paranormal shows, but says that's never been the case with the shows he's been involved with.

"That's probably a reason why my shows aren't on anymore," he says.

On *Ghost Hunters International*, it was Bradford's job to be in charge of technology and evidence. And he says there was pressure by producers to hold on to everything and use EVPs even when no one could validate whether or not they were legitimate or just background sounds. The reasoning was the team needed to find some kind of evidence each show.

"That's fair, but at the same time, we're not going to present something that isn't something," says Bradford.

He cites his position on evidence, and some prima-donna behaviour from a fellow team member, as the reason *Ghost Hunters International* isn't on the air anymore. Bradford says the team didn't find ghosts all the time, and was also able to debunk a lot of stories and alleged activity at many locations. The problem was that didn't play well on television.

"A lot of the debunking was scrapped from the show," he says.

Why scrap material like that, when debunking alleged activity is a cherished practice for any serious paranormal investigator? Bradford says the number of paranormal investigators among the average television viewing audience is minuscule.

"The majority of people who watch ghost TV are not paranormal investigators. So yes, for the other investigators, that's great, but other people watch the shows because they want to see ghosts, and that is the problem. That's where you get the fine line between 'Is that entertainment, or is that real'," says Bradford.

To appease the investigator in him, as well as the network, Bradford did his best to keep things real. He says being possessed by a demon every week on television hurts one's credibility, which is why he never felt compelled to go down that route.

Trending Fear, his most recent series, was a bit different. That series was based on experiences New York resident, and former BuzzFeed writer and illustrator, Adam Ellis had after capturing the image of a ghost child in his apartment. Ellis chronicled his experiences on social media under the hashtag DearDavid, which allowed people to follow his experiences in real time.

Ellis was approached by the Travel Channel to travel North America helping others understand their haunting experiences. Bradford joined the team as the veteran investigator, and he says the desire wasn't just to have a camera team document the investigations, but to be a part of them.

"Our camera crew, we got them involved. We broke that fourth wall because they were experiencing stuff, so that validated other things," says Bradford.

"The audience isn't stupid. They know there's a camera crew there, so they were just as much a part of it as we were."

The six-episode first season of *Trending Fear* debuted just before the COVID-19 pandemic hit North America. Bradford isn't sure if there will be a second at this point.

Asking someone like Bradford, who has had such varied experiences and used – not to mention created – so much equipment for the paranormal field, what his favourite piece of gear is might seem like a strange question. But he does indeed have one that stands out above the rest, and that is Boo Buddy.

Boo Buddy is an interactive, ghost-hunting bear Bradford built. Boo Buddy talks and asks EVP questions, detects changes in electromagnetic fields, temperature, movement and vibration, and responds to each in turn with a cute, friendly voice.

"It's still one of a kind. You see all these copycat people trying to make what we made, and nothing even comes close," he says. "You can put a K2 meter up a bear's ass, but it's still not the same."

What keeps Bradford investigating after all these years? He says it's not money, fame or women, because he's not famous, is broke, and married. It comes back to that interest in science fiction and a desire to be James Bond or Indiana Jones when he grows up.

"To be quite honest, I'm a nerd," Bradford says. "I kind of enjoy the fact I can disassociate myself from real-world stuff. It's the same thing as submerging yourself into a computer game."

And if he has his way, Bradford will be exploring strange new worlds, and have exciting adventures in far-off places, for many years to come.

3 KEN GERHARD

When meeting someone new, it's not uncommon for one of the first questions asked to be "what do you do for a living?" What is uncommon is the response Ken Gerhard gives.

"I'm honored to be a widely regarded cryptozoologist. Which means I investigate evidence of unknown animals."

Indeed, Gerhard spends his days researching and seeking out strange beasts that haven't been proven by mainstream science. His life is about the pursuit of legendary creatures like Bigfoot and the Loch Ness Monster and their many related "cousins" around the globe, as well as lesser known – and not quite as exotic – specimens, including the ivory-billed woodpecker, which was thought extinct in the 1930s but sightings persist to this day.

"It's a pretty broad field," says Gerhard. "Sometimes it gets into some weird, fringe areas like Mothman, as an example, or the chupacabra or Dogman; kind of these phantoms or kind of metaphysical types of creatures.

"It's a rather unconventional thing to do with my life."

An unconventional thing Gerhard has fully embraced. His home office in San Antonio, Texas, is full of photographs, sketches, and mock-up models of the beings he's spent twenty years of his life researching and, as is often the case, physically tracking in the wild; be it hiking through the dense wilderness of the Pacific Northwest or by boat on a Scottish loch.

On one wall is a map of the United States marked with what could possibly be the migratory patterns of winged creatures called Thunderbirds and pterosaurs – winged reptilian creatures with leathery, bat-like wings that were supposed to have gone extinct sixty-five million years ago but are still reported today. The sightings, marked in red lines, flow from north to south across the map, stretching from Alaska down past Texas.

And of course there's the plaster casts of alleged Bigfoot prints, which Gerhard has gathered from all over the world. They come in various shapes and sizes. One is reportedly from a Sasquatch that appears to have had a crippled foot. This is marked by a sizable protrusion of what Gerhard suspects to be bone, which makes the print unique and, in his opinion, legitimate.

"Why would someone go to the effort of making a fake footprint of a crippled foot?" he asks.

Another cast shows a partial print with toes, markings that suggest to Gerhard something large stepped through the mud. He shows off the toe markings, which indeed look like the toes slid through the mud as opposed to stepped down hard.

Gerhard looks the part. He's frequently seen, be it at conventions or during television appearances, wearing dark clothing, often grey or black, with prints depicting the creatures he's spent a good portion of his life searching for. And he usually sports a trimmed beard and a black leather cowboy hat emblazoned with a mean-looking skull.

Much like paranormal investigation, cryptozoology is a pseudoscience that aims to prove the existence of things believed to be folklore, in this case animals. And, as with investigating and researching ghosts, science has yet to embrace the findings of those who research the phenomena due to a lack of hard scientific evidence. So far, nothing found by cryptozoologists like Gerhard can be quantified and tested in a lab. But the hope among these researchers and investigators is one day they will find something that will get science's attention.

Like many a paranormal investigator or cryptozoologist, Gerhard's interest in the subject was sparked at an early age. As a boy, he was interested in "animals, creatures, and monsters" and was either blessed, or cursed, with a vivid imagination. He had pet snakes and baby alligators and enjoyed watching Scooby-Doo cartoons and the early Godzilla movies whenever they came on TV.

His father was a scientist, and his mother was adventurous and liked to travel, so he had a variety of influences on his young mind. This resulted in the rationality of science mixed with a spirit of adventure and heading off to places unknown.

The eureka moment came when Gerhard was eight years old, and he caught a short news segment about Bigfoot on television.

"Something just clicked," he says.

The segment featured the famous Patterson-Gimlin film, showed a group of Bigfoot hunters in the woods, and displayed plaster casts of footprints. Gerhard remembers it well, decades later.

As a result, he spent a lot of time at the library, reading everything he could on the subject of Sasquatch and the yeti. If a documentary came on TV about Bigfoot, or any monster really, Gerhard would watch it.

He vividly remembers a trip to the Minnesota State Fair in 1976, where he saw an exhibit of the Minnesota Ice Man; a Bigfoot-like creature found frozen in a block of ice. The Minnesota Ice Man has since become a famous find in the field of cryptozoology and stoked the fires of imagination in Gerhard at the time.

And, when travelling with his mom, he would investigate and research whatever strange, legendary creature was believed to stalk the country or region, he says.

"In Australia it was the Bunyip, In Switzerland the Tatzelwurm. I travelled to South America and Africa. By the time I was fifteen I was at Loch Ness with my father on a fishing trip. I didn't spend much time fishing, I was patrolling the loch with an eight-millimetre movie camera and interviewing people about what they thought the monster was," says Gerhard.

"It was a series of things like that – epiphanies – as I look back on my life that always kind of stoked the fire and kept the passion and fire for cryptozoology burning."

Although he approached the subject with the enthusiasm of a professional, Gerhard never thought he'd make cryptozoology his life's work. He says his mother always steered him toward being a writer or archeologist. Instead, his life took an interesting side road, and he spent twenty years as a touring musician, producing records and travelling around the country with different bands.

Naturally, he used these tours as an opportunity to investigate various legendary creature sightings like the Beast of Bray Road, a werewolf-like creature spotted on a rural road outside of Elkhorn, Wisconsin, in 1936 and then during the 1990s.

"Wherever we were, when we had a day off on tour, I'd steer the band toward some location where I could do an investigation," he says.

Gerhard started to approach cryptozoology from a more professional standpoint in the early 2000s, when the Internet made it possible for him to connect with other Bigfoot researchers in Texas. This allowed him to attend conventions with like-minded people and join expeditions in search of his favourite cryptid.

"My passion intensified, and then I started writing books based on the advice of Loren Coleman, who's a leading cryptozoologist," he said.

The books led to lectures, which eventually led Gerhard to his first television show, which was a Bigfoot episode of *Legend Hunters* for the Canadian Travel Channel.

"I've just been very blessed, very lucky, that things have just taken off since then," he says.

When investigating anything paranormal, the hardest part is actually capturing evidence of its existence, be it a ghost or Sasquatch. And even then, what one does get on camera, or record on audio, isn't going to stand up in a court of law. The majority of the time, a ghostly apparition or strange hump in the water materializes to the naked eye, but disappears as soon as cameras roll, or turns up right after the equipment is put away.

Gerhard is honest about his actual cryptid encounters, saying he's never actually been able to confirm the existence of one with his own eyes. But he has had a few personal experiences that he can't explain. As is often the case, it's the personal experiences – unexplained events that happen to you but were not witnessed by others – that drive an investigator forward.

As a young boy, his family lived in Minnesota, and there was a small lake behind his family's home. He recounts one time when he was sitting in the backyard, staring at the lake, and swears he saw a hump rise out of the water.

"It was like the classic Nessie hump," he says, in reference to the Loch Ness Monster. "Even at that young age, I knew there was no way that something like that could live in this lake. It was so small. But I was still just fixated on this hump."

Although eight or nine at the time, Gerhard was aware enough to realize there weren't any boats on the water, or other objects that could have caused this hump to appear, at least to his young eyes. The hump eventually disappeared back beneath the surface, and young Gerhard tried to explain away what he saw as an optical illusion.

"But still, it got my imagination stirring. What was that hump? What could it have been?"

He had a far more dramatic encounter with some... thing many years later, when Gerhard joined Chester Moore Jr., a wildlife tracker and author, and other Bigfoot researchers on an investigation at Cottonwood Lake in North Texas. The group had heard of some recent sightings – including one that scared a group of campers out of the woods – and were going to investigate. Gerhard naturally took Moore Jr. up on the invitation.

The remote lake was a four-or five-hour drive from Gerhard's home and took the team down a fifteen-mile gravel road to what seemed like the middle of nowhere. He says the plan was to camp out and explore the area in search of tracks and other evidence.

Just after dark on the first night, the hunters were doing a perimeter search around the lake. Gerhard was armed with a Sony camera equipped with early night vision that he was using to document the investigation.

"And suddenly we heard something grunting at us," he says. "I recorded it on the audio on the camera. It was pretty dark, so I didn't get a good shot of much else."

To Gerhard, the grunting sounded like a primate. He says everyone stopped moving and looked at each other. Several F-bombs were also dropped.

"None of us could identify this as any known animal that we were familiar with," says Gerhard. "What I tell people is it sounded like grunting, panting, like heavy breathing, and also like laughter."

No one could see the culprit, given it was dark and they were in heavy brush, but the group assumed whatever made the sound was very large and very powerful based on how loud it was. Gerhard says the hairs were literally standing up on the back of his neck because of how aggressive and scary the sounds were.

Moore Jr. was the only one armed with a weapon, his shotgun. He decided he was going to flush whatever the thing was out and started crawling through the brush on his belly with the shotgun. Gerhard decided to work his way around to where he figured the animal would go running when Moore Jr. sprang into action. If it was a Bigfoot or other legendary beast, he wanted to get it on film as it ran away.

"Forget the Patterson-Gimlin film. This could be the Gerhard film!" he says. "Or this could be my last act on Earth, and I'll become famous for capturing found footage of this thing pummeling me."

Despite Moore Jr.'s best efforts, he couldn't get the animal to budge, so everyone decided to try a different tactic. Gerhard says they relocated to a levy overlooking the lake and trained a million-candle-power spotlight on the brush where the noises came from. To everyone's surprise, and delight, they saw some yellowish green eyeshine looking back at them.

The eyeshine was well off the ground, confirming whatever it was – be it deer, bear or Bigfoot – was a big animal, he says.

"It was hard to tell. Is that it, or a deer?" he remembers saying. "There's definitely eyes looking at us!"

They remained in that spot for a while, then decided to set up camp for the night, opting to locate themselves near where they saw the eyeshine and heard the animal. Gerhard remembers everyone's adrenalin was pumping, but this was what they were there for.

Throughout the course of the night, the team heard what Gerhard describes as "a creepy, moaning sound" coming from across the lake. He says it could have been a cow, but at the same time, didn't sound quite like a cow.

Gerhard had a megaphone with him and started mimicking the sound to the best of his ability in order to communicate with it. He would duplicate the moan, and whatever it was would answer back, he says.

"That was creepy."

The back-and-forth continued for a long time before everyone got too tired to stay awake, and eventually they curled up in their sleeping bags and went to sleep. Gerhard says nothing happened the rest of the night, but the next morning, they did find some interesting bits of evidence to validate their experience from the night before.

"We finally had our courage up, and we hacked our way through this brush where we heard this thing, and there was a little beach on the side of the lake when we made it through the brush," he says. "And there were some very deep, human-shaped footprints! They weren't enormous, but they were very deep."

The sand made the imprints vague and a little messy, but the men could follow them through the sand to the water's edge. There they found several large turtle shells that had been ripped in half from top to bottom and left in a pile. He likens the discovery to a pile of pistachio or peanut shells left on a barroom floor.

"There was no flesh left on the shells at all. They were just the shells," says Gerhard. "I've owned many turtles in my life, and I can't imagine anything actually ripping a turtle in half."

When he puts all those things together – the vocalization, the eyeshine, the footprints, the turtle shells – Gerhard believes he encountered something unknown that could possibly have been a Bigfoot or a Sasquatch.

This was the closest encounter Gerhard has had in the woods. During his many other adventures, he's heard grunts and other vocalizations, and perhaps one tree knock, which is believed to be how Sasquatch communicate or warn others off their territory.

As paranormal investigators, we have several tools to aid in our quest for ghostly evidence, the most common being digital recorders, motion and still cameras, and the

Spirit Box, which uses AM/FM frequencies to try to "tune in" to spirits' voices. But what does a cryptozoologist use when venturing out into the field, especially considering his prey is likely a living, breathing animal that could do him and his colleagues harm? Never mind the woods and wilds of North America have very real, and at times very dangerous, beasts to worry about.

Gerhard has friends who are ghost hunters and UFO researchers, and he says there's some similarities between the occupations. In fact, he jokingly believes the best thing about the field of study is all the toys.

Cameras – especially stationary devices like trail cameras – are commonly used. Trail cameras are effective because they can be set up on trees and left for hours, or even days, at a time, taking pictures or shooting video whenever movement is detected. Most are equipped with infrared to pick up heat sources in the dark.

"We use those a lot," he says, adding he usually carries a camera with him as well.

Night vision is also a key tool in Gerhard's trade. He always brings a pair of night-vision goggles with him and, being an "old-school guy", he prefers to use the first-generation devices.

"If you can afford it, a lot of the guys use thermal imaging," he says. This functions like infrared and is effective at picking up heat sources in the wild.

Just like the paranormal field, cryptozoologists use audio recorders to capture sounds and vocalizations. Gerhard also uses a call blaster, which is a battery-powered speaker with preprogrammed animal sounds and distress calls he can broadcast out into the woods in hope of luring his quarry to him.

"It's like hunting. We use a lot of the same things we use as hunters," he says, adding he brings binoculars and GPS with him as well.

Collecting DNA has also become an important part of the cryptozoologist's work. The hope is hair, skin, or even blood evidence can be found and brought back to a lab for testing. So far, much of what has been collected and believed to belong to a Bigfoot or Dogman has turned out to be a hoax or DNA from an existing animal. But Gerhard carries DNA swab kits with him just in case.

And, as one might expect, Gerhard always has casting materials on hand in case he comes across any tracks in the wild. He personally uses dental stone powder that's used for making imprints of teeth. All he has to do is add water, and the mix does a fine job of capturing any print.

"It's like plaster but better," he says. "You can tell a lot about an animal by looking at the track and its morphology."

These are the more common tools in a cryptozoologist's tool belt, but there's definitely some... shall we say... unique equipment at Gerhard's disposal as well. How unique? How about a gallon of mountain lion urine?

No, Gerhard doesn't go out and follow mountain lions around, waiting for them to pee. He says there's a business in the Dakotas that sells mountain lion urine online. He has no idea where they get it, and doesn't want to know. But the urine makes for a great lure for big cats like panthers and cougars, and Gerhard uses it when prowling for phantom cats.

Phantom cats, also known as Alien Big Cats, have been reported for more than a hundred years, and all over the world. People have seen cougars, jaguars, leopards and other exotic cats outside their indigenous range, including sightings of the creatures themselves, or found evidence of their tracks or attacks on prey.

Gerhard has even gone so far as to collect mountain lion feces out of an enclosure in his efforts to find a suitable lure for these phantom cats.

"Those are some of the weird things that I might deploy, but not too often," he says.

When it comes to aquatic cryptids like the Loch Ness Monster in Scotland, or Ogopogo in British Columbia, Canada, the equipment required is understandably much more expensive. Devices like side-scan sonar, which provides him a view of a body of water beneath the surface, and an underwater camera equipped with a fifty-foot cable can cost thousands of dollars. His underwater camera is capable of filming in infrared.

"There's a lot of different gadgets and toys that we use in the field of cryptozoology," says Gerhard. "It makes it a lot of fun."

Oh, and Gerhard also packs a 12-gauge pump-action shotgun when he's in the field, but it's not for Bigfoot, which he has no intention of ever harming. When out in the field, especially in his home state of Texas, there's plenty of other things in the wild that can do one harm, like wild pigs, snakes, mountain lions, and bears.

When it comes to the validity of the creatures he's investigating, Gerhard believes there's enough evidence to convince him and other cryptozoologists to keep hunting. He has his map of winged cryptid migration and some six thousand documented sightings of Bigfoot or Sasquatch-like creatures in North America, many of which he considers credible.

There's a pattern to the Bigfoot sightings, he says. Many are in the Pacific Northwest, ranging from Alaska through British Columbia, Canada, into Washington State, Oregon and California. Most are in mountainous terrain, he says. In the Eastern United States, there are concentrations of Bigfoot and Sasquatch in wilderness regions, including Texas, Louisiana, and Arkansas. Florida also has a lot of sightings, as do Ohio and Kentucky.

Much like the Thunderbird and pterosaur sightings, Gerhard has maps showing every credible Bigfoot sighting up on his walls.

When it comes to aquatic creatures, Gerhard believes he's also found a pattern. He says there are dozens of lake monsters reported around the world, and from Loch Ness to Lake Okanagan to Lake Champlain, he's noticed the lakes are all along the same line of latitude, between thirty and fifty degrees north.

"They're all very similar types of lakes," he says. "They're all cold, glacial lakes that were carved out by glacial retreats. Similar water temperatures stocked by similar species of salmonid fish like trout and salmon. So, that's interesting to me."

The water in all these lakes is also peaty and dark, with poor visibility, he says.

Gerhard believes many, if not most, of the animals he's spent his life researching and hunting are as-yet-confirmed-by-science species that will one day be proven as real. He says it's only a matter of time and effort. But what does he think of the more metaphysical creatures people are seeing like the Mothman, a bizarre winged creature many believe to be a portent to some pending disaster?

The Mothman was first spotted outside Point Pleasant, Virginia, and was seen for thirteen months before the Ohio River Bridge collapsed, killing dozens of people.

If Mothman and other supernatural cryptids do exist, Gerhard believes they are some kind of metaphysical construct and not flesh-and-blood beings that evolved on this planet that will be found in any zoological or fossil record.

He says there's a lot of "weird elements" that surround these sightings in terms of appearance and behaviour, including, in some cases, forms of spiritual attachment that follow witnesses home, resulting in poltergeist-like behaviour.

"I'm not sure what they are," he says. "Honestly, I think that whole concept is completely beyond our current level of understanding."

One theory Gerhard has heard that could provide an answer to such sightings is these beings are projections from the recesses of the unconscious minds of those who see them. He says this could also be why people see ghosts, and why spirits and beings like Mothman seem so keen to interact with us.

When it comes to cryptids Gerhard would like to investigate, but hasn't had the chance to, he says he'd love to spend time at Lake Okanagan in search of Canada's own Loch Ness Monster, Ogopogo.

One thing is for certain, no matter where Gerhard goes, he'll bring his years of experience, his trademark hat, and the enthusiasm and open mind that's served him since he was a boy, watching that Bigfoot story on the news all those years ago.

4   DAVE GIBB

It wasn't being a part of a spiritual family, with a mother who formed her own spiritualist movement, that led Dave Gibb to being a paranormal investigator.

It was martial arts.

Granted, there's a spiritual aspect to martial arts. But Gibb, who founded the Canadian Haunting and Paranormal Society in Pembroke, Ontario, fell into investigating by accident while travelling in the United States with his sensei, or martial arts instructor.

The duo was on the competitive circuit and found themselves near Gettysburg one night.

"It was an off road. It wasn't like it was a major site you'd see when you were down there," he says. "And what we saw, what we envisioned we were seeing, was a lantern being carried down a hill, and getting closer to the car."

There was a sudden flash of light inside the car, like a spark from a flint-lock rifle going off near the steering wheel, says Gibb.

"It smelled like gunpowder," he says.

The two well-trained men jumped out of their seats, and Gibb's sensei put the car in gear and sped away. They fled in such a panic, his sensei didn't even bother to turn the headlights on. Gibb jokes the two men almost became ghosts themselves.

Although the experience left him badly shaken, it stuck with Gibb. He decided then and there that he wanted to learn more about what happened to him and his instructor that night.

The battle at Gettysburg was a major turning point during the American Civil War, and claimed the lives of more than three thousand people. Ever since, residents and tourists alike have reported seeing everything from single ghosts to spooky lights to experiencing ethereal "recreations" of the battle itself. Gibb suspects this was what he and his sensei experienced that night, and he's returned to

Gettysburg many times since during his twenty-seven years as a paranormal investigator.

"I used to go down there and spend months there. I've probably been down there fifteen or sixteen times since."

His most recent visit occurred two years ago, and Gibb had his wife and daughter with him. He recalls he and his wife, Sandy, scampering through the fields at night, following a sound she'd heard. Gibb says it suddenly seemed like they were being surrounded, and the noise of movement was as loud as "a pack of elephants".

Almost everything he encounters at Gettysburg is experience based, meaning it's encounters he and whoever is with him have that can't be taken as evidence. Gibb has tried rolling audio and shooting video, but all he manages to pick up with his recorders are the mosquitoes and other bugs buzzing around. He says the bugs are so thick at times, that's all he can see when shooting video too.

"I gotta say it's the one place I go to that every time I go, I have an experience," he says, adding he encounters something either on a former field of battle, or at the Colton, a hotel he stays at.

While at the Colton, Gibb has awoken to the sound of troops marching up and down the hallway, and has seen guards appear in his room, he says.

"Could that have been a facility of me waking up weird? Yeah, possibly. But it felt really real," says Gibb.

His first Gettysburg experience occurred in 1994, and he investigated on an informal basis for eleven years before forming Canadian Haunting Paranormal Society (C.H.A.P.S.) in 2005. He currently operates two

C.H.A.P.S. offices in the Greater Toronto area, and another in the Ottawa Valley four hours away. He's done countless residential investigations since, and has also investigated at commercial and historic sites all over North America, including several renowned haunted locations in the United States.

Like any investigator, Gibb has his personal favourite investigation; one that sticks out above all the rest. He makes a point of saying he's had many that produced a lot of evidence, or at least evidence from a paranormal investigation standpoint. But in terms of the best all-around experience he and his team have had, he ranks West Virginia State Penitentiary at the top of the list.

West Virginia State Penitentiary can best be described as a gothic-style former prison located in Moundsville, West Virginia. It operated from 1876 to 1995, and is now a tourist attraction and training facility.

It's also rumoured to be haunted, and has become a popular location for ghost hunters and dark tourists.

The reality series MTV's *Fear* put West Virginia State Penitentiary on the map, so to speak. The show had contestants spend two nights at an allegedly haunted location, completing dares in an effort to prove if the location was haunted or not. The show's pilot and first regular episode filmed there, and several other paranormal reality series have descended on the location since.

The prison was home to violent offenders, and has seen its share of violence, including riots. It's also said to be built on top of the Adena Native Americans' sacred burial grounds. Dark, shadowy figures have been seen wandering the halls and cell blocks, and investigators have claimed to capture various EVPs (electronic voice phenomena) including shotgun blasts, strange sounds, and screams.

"It's great. It's the setting for a murder, really," Gibb says of West Virginia State Penitentiary. "It's an ominous-looking building."

Gibb has brought C.H.A.P.S. members to the site on a couple of occasions, and says everybody had one kind of experience or another during their stay.

He recalls conversing with another investigator via two-way radio. Gibb was at one end of the building, and the investigator was at the other, in the mental ward, which was easily just over half a mile away.

"We were about as far away from each other as one gets," he says.

Screams would transmit through the radio from time to time, and Gibb even caught the screams on video he shot during the night, he says. Both he and the other investigator heard them, and neither could trace the screams back to any source. They seemed to resonate from the radio's frequency.

A while later, Gibb and a teammate found themselves in the mental ward, which is accessed via two sets of stairs, one on one side of the ward, the other opposite it. Some of the stairs are so dilapidated the concrete has worn away, leaving only the metal supports.

BOOM, BOOM.

Gibb says he heard loud, banging footsteps coming up one set of stairs like "some eight-hundred-pound beast" was walking up one of the sets of stairs and slamming its foot on each one. The team could hear it get closer and closer to the door.

"Even as an investigator, the physical side of things has to come across. It was fight-or-flight syndrome," he says, adding he and the team slowly backed away from that doorway to the other end of the ward.

No sooner did they get to the other side of the mental ward, than they heard the same pounding footsteps coming at them from that staircase!

"Those are two totally different ways to access the ward," says Gibb. "You couldn't go up one and run down and go up the other. You'd have to bypass through other parts of the jail first."

That same night, one of Gibb's investigators had a colony of bats swoop right past her, and she let out a scream that shook everyone to his or her core. At that point, Gibb decided it was time for everyone to go outside and have a smoke, he says.

"There was a level of tension that just doesn't exist at most times," he says, and laughs. "So the scariest thing on that investigation, was her."

But that's not all Gibb and his C.H.A.P.S. investigators experienced at West Virginia State Penitentiary. One time the team was in the north range, which is where death-row inmates were held while they awaited execution. Gibb says many people have reported being touched or prodded by unseen hands there.

Gibb says investigators don't have access to the full range because the top floors are caged off, but that doesn't mean the activity is in any way diminished. In fact, there were times the investigators found themselves chasing some... thing along the top of the cage from one end of the range to the other.

When telling the story to people, some scoff and say they were simply chasing wildlife that had made its way into the prison. Gibb isn't so sure that's the case.

"It had a definite impression like it was human," he says.

Even more dramatic was an experience Gibb and his wife had in that range. They found themselves locked in a heated debate during the investigation and soon found themselves being pelted by rocks from above.

To put this in context, Gibb and his wife weren't standing together, but were in fact ten feet apart, he says. The shower of stones covered the entire area, and bounced through the wires of the cage and hit them.

"It's just an incredible place," he says.

Only a hardened paranormal investigator would call an experience like that incredible. Most people would've run for the hills and never returned, whether the culprits be ghosts or otherwise.

The C.H.A.P.S. team returned with members of C.O.P.S., or Correctional Officers Paranormal Society. C.O.P.S. is exactly what it sounds like; a group of paranormal investigators who are also current or former prison guards. Gibb says having that group on-site didn't make the investigation any less frightening.

"It was just as scary to hear them scream and holler as it was us," says Gibb.

Both teams experienced strange electrical activity

during that investigation, including video monitors switching off on their own, he says. They also recorded power coming from a water cooler in the prison's cafeteria. The cooling system was on, using hydro and pumping Freon despite the fact the machine wasn't plugged in.

Like many personal experiences, the lack of physical evidence can be frustrating. Gibb recounts a time he and two other investigators thought they captured the image of a shadow being with not one, but two cameras, as it came up a flight of stairs toward them. He says the shadow looked tangible, but the two pictures make it look like it might have been caused by one of the team, even though they weren't moving in such a way to give the impression of the shadow coming at them.

"The picture we took wasn't reliable, but what we saw was," he says. "We debated that one for years."

Even though the penitentiary has provided some of his most memorable investigations, Gibb has had a couple other experiences stand out over the more than two hundred cases he and C.H.A.P.S. have taken on. One occurred while investigating a property in Ashmore, Illinois, where the team heard a piano being played despite there being no one to play it. Gibb, his wife, and another investigator heard this, and even captured it on audio.

"That was neat," he said.

The other occurred one night at a medical facility that he's not at liberty to name. Gibb and another investigator were seated at a picnic table in the middle of a hallway that connected to some seventy-five rooms. He says they were sitting quietly and on the lookout for any activity.

The other investigator, Adrian, suddenly stirred, like he'd seen something. "Did... did you see?" Adrian said to Gibb.

Gibb says he thought he saw a human-like shadow move in the hallway, but there was nothing that could have caused there to be such a thing. The next thing he knew, he was chasing after it down the hallway.

"My head is down, and I'm chasing after feet. I'm looking at the feet because they seem to be the brightest part," he says.

He chased the shadow some three hundred to four hundred meters into a room, and he remembers believing Adrian was right behind him the whole time.

Then he turned around, and Adrian was still sitting at the picnic table!

"Adrian is a football field away from me," he says. "That was the first time I'd ever had that happen. That was a weird event for me."

But the spookiest of personal experiences occurred at a mansion in Smith's Grove, Ontario. The mansion was being used as a funeral parlour, and Gibb, who was training to be a funeral director at the time, found himself alone in a room with two coffins in it.

Gibb was seated quietly, taking in the environment, when he felt a breeze blow by, like someone moving past him, unseen.

Then he heard a whisper, he says, followed by movement, like someone had sat down beside him.

"I'm now getting the willies a little bit," says Gibb.

All of a sudden, a lid falls off one of the coffins onto the floor.

Gibb says he ran so fast he slammed into the door on the way out, dislocating his shoulder.

Typical for a moment like this, the team had a video camera rolling in the room that would have captured everything... but for reasons unknown, the camera didn't work that night.

"Which is good and bad. I always give the team shit for doing things like that. For running. And I ran out of there fast," says Gibb. "So it didn't catch me."

When it comes to equipment, Gibb has some favourites, especially when investigating facilities as vast as West Virginia State Penitentiary. He likes to set up static and video cameras. He carries a video camera with him, but not to film the investigation. He likes to film the team in case anyone tries to stage or fake evidence, or even does something to unintentionally cause something to happen that could be perceived as paranormal.

C.H.A.P.S. also runs multiple audio recorders during a night's work, and breaks out motion detectors as well, says Gibb.

He's even used experimental equipment like proximity light panels, which use infrared to detect motion, and light up in response to it. He picked the panels up because he saw them used on an episode of Nick Groff's *Paranormal Lockdown*, but wouldn't use them on a regular basis.

"It was one of those stupid purchases I made because I saw it on TV and thought it looked cool," says Gibb. "We've all done it."

Like many investigators, Gibb prefers to stick with tried-and-true devices like cameras and audio recorders. He says a lot of the new tools being invented for ghost hunting are untested and can be easily influenced by air movement and electrical interference. Audio and video falls under enough scrutiny because of the number of proven hoaxes in the paranormal field.

What does Gibb think these encounters are? Do paranormal investigators make contact with the dead? Or are they "recordings", for lack of a better word, caused by our energy leaving the body after we die? Or are they beings from some other dimension?

He answers with one more story. He and the team investigated a haunting at a family home, and became good friends with the family who lived there. Sadly, the husband, Dave, died of a heart attack. At the request of the wife, Gibb and his team went back one more time to see if they could make contact with Dave.

Gibb ended up doing an EVP session on his own in an upstairs room while the other two teammates, who were female, were downstairs with the wife. He had a video camera set up and pointed at himself.

"I said, 'Okay, Dave. You need to speak to me'," he says. "And all I got was a male voice saying, 'I want to come home.' Clear as day."

The video is focused on Gibb, and his mouth doesn't move. And there wasn't another male in the house at that time. Gibb played the video for the family, and they believe it sounds like Dave. Gibb says the voice sounds like the man he knew and met several times.

Being a paranormal investigator can be tiring, unrewarding, and gruelling work. Most of the time, you get nothing. But Gibb says moments like hearing Dave's voice make the effort worthwhile, and keep him coming back for more.

5   JASON MURPHY AND DOUG MOMBOURQUETTE

Left: Jason Murphy, Right: Doug Mombourquette

Sitting down with Haunts from the Cape founders Jason Murphy and Doug Mombourquette, it's readily apparent these guys enjoy what they do, be it shooting the breeze with friends, or hunting ghosts.

The duo is located on Cape Breton Island in Nova Scotia, Canada. Sydney, Nova Scotia, to be exact. If you listen, there's a "hint of Eastern Canadian" in their accents, Mombourquette more so than Murphy.

"You have to use many words to describe where we're at," says Murphy.

"If you're from Cape Breton, you don't say you're from Nova Scotia," Mombourquette adds.

"We don't want to be associated with the mainlanders," Murphy says, prompting good-natured laughter from the two of them. "It's that island mentality."

Murphy and Mombourquette laugh a lot while describing their exploits in the paranormal. They've been investigating ghosts and hauntings since 2014, but have had an interest long before. Murphy's interest spiked as a kid, when he heard about his great-uncle who died in World War II. This prompted Murphy to question what happens to us when we die, he says.

He also grew up on a steady diet of television shows like *Unsolved Mysteries*, which left him sleeping with the light on and "scaring the crap out of myself".

"There wasn't one specific thing that got me going," he says. "I've always loved it."

Like Murphy, Mombourquette has been interested in the subject since he was a boy. But that interest peaked in the summer of 1996 while working at the Keltic Lodge at the Highlands in Ingonish, Cape Breton. The lodge is a hotel/spa/golf resort bordering Cape Breton National Park and the Atlantic Ocean. And, like many older buildings in Cape Breton and Eastern Canada, it has its fair share of ghost stories attached to it.

The lodge is located on a peninsula overlooking the

ocean, and on this particular night, a hurricane was blowing by the island. Mombourquette says the waves were so fierce he could reach out over the end of the peninsula and feel the ocean spray, despite how high up he was.

He and his girlfriend at the time – she's now his wife – were watching the storm. Something caught her attention, and she pointed down to the bottom of the cliff, he says.

"There's a man down there standing on the cliff," she said to him.

Mombourquette told her she was crazy. There was no way down, and the storm would make any climb impossible. But he looked anyway, and sure enough, there was a man standing down there, the waves crashing around him, he says.

"He was dressed in old-time clothes. Like with a cape with red felt inside it. It was period clothing," he says.

Mombourquette and his girlfriend yelled at him, thinking he might need help. The man heard them, looked up, and simply nodded back, he says.

"And when the next wave was about to hit, he vanished before it hit," says Mombourquette.

The couple went back to the lodge and told the story to the staff on duty. The locals knew right away whom they'd seen, saying it was the Vampire of Ingonish. Mombourquette says this "vampire" had been showing up at various locales in the area all that summer.

"Someone would say they'd pick him up [from the side of the road]; then he'd disappear from the car. He'd walk out in front of people, and they'd drive straight through him," says Mombourquette. "So that's what really piqued my interest in the paranormal."

From the moment he learned of the Vampire of Ingonish, Mombourquette wanted to start his own paranormal investigation group. But that didn't happen until he met Murphy.

Murphy and Mombourquette didn't become friends until they started Haunts from the Cape, but they were acquainted with each other prior. Mombourquette worked in the stock-room at the local Superstore, and Murphy was "the milk guy", a milkman who occasionally worked at that store.

"I managed the back shift and used to let him into the store," says Mombourquette. "I was his keys."

"I'd have my morning cigarette and coffee and then ring the buzzer. Doug would be the guy who let me in," says Murphy.

So what brought these two together to form a paranormal investigation team? Murphy posted something about the paranormal online. He can't remember what, or where. Mombourquette saw the post and replied.

"Doug messaged me and said, 'You're into that stuff?' I said, 'Yeah.' He said, 'Wanna start a group?' I was like, 'Yeah, let's do it'," says Murphy.

The first order of business was equipment. Murphy told Mombourquette he couldn't afford to buy any equipment.

"I can't afford it either, but my Visa can," Mombourquette remembers saying.

The rest is, as they say, history.

The duo has had several memorable investigations in the six years Haunts from the Cape has been active, but Murphy and Mombourquette each have their own favourite personal experience. For Mombourquette, it occurred at Duhaget house in the unincorporated community of Louisbourg on Cape Breton Island.

Louisburg was a French fortress built on the home of the Mi'kmaq First Nations, and was the centre of French colonial life in early Canada from 1713 to 1758. The Duhaget property belonged to Robert Tarride Duhaget, who was garrison commander at Louisbourg for the duration.

According to Mombourquette and Murphy, the fortress at Louisbourg is the most haunted place in Cape Breton and has been the site of many investigations. Haunts from the Cape's YouTube channel includes some thirty videos documenting ghostly activity at the historic site. The site was the scene of much violence and death, which lends itself to hauntings.

Duhaget House is now a museum depicting French life in the 1700s, and also has miniature displays recreating battles from the era. Mombourquette says he was bent down, pulling equipment out of a bag, when he felt a tap on the shoulder.

"I turned around right quick, thinking it was Jason looking for batteries," he says. "And, when I looked over, he was one room over."

Murphy asked him what was wrong, and Mombourquette told him he'd been tapped on the shoulder. He says there wasn't anyone else in the room.

"That was pretty cool for me, that way," he says.

How about Murphy? He too has a standout personal experience. His took place in Sydney Mines in Cape Breton, which has a rich history of coal production. The site was actually used to support British loyalists during the American Revolution.

Murphy says there's a decommissioned church at Sydney Mines that was purchased by a family from Ontario. The main floor was left empty, but the basement was turned into a daycare. The children in care there told staff they kept seeing an apparition of a woman, and drew pictures of what looked like a nun.

"The children kept seeing her coming through walls and disappearing," says Murphy.

Some research revealed a priest once impregnated a nun, and the nun killed herself, says Murphy. Two weeks after her death, the priest was found dead at the bottom of the staircase to the basement. Why did that happen? No one has ever found out.

Mombourquette says the owners saw the spirit of a priest wandering about the property on more than one occasion.

The Haunts from the Cape team investigated, starting in the daycare and working their way upstairs onto the main floor, where all that remains of the original layout are the confessional booths. Murphy found himself alone, and walking down a hall toward the back of the building. He had his phone out and was recording audio on it.

BANG!

The sound came from the end of the hall, where no

one else was. Murphy noticed his hand start to shake, and he was "freaked out", he says. Instead of continuing down the hall, he turned back toward the rest of the team, to see what they were up to.

Equally as creepy was the church attic, where he and Mombourquette captured some compelling EVPs, including a voice they can only describe as a "demon voice" saying the word "priest".

"When the word 'priest' came through, it was pretty harsh sounding," says Mombourquette. "It wasn't a normal, regular EVP. It was very harsh."

He says the confessional booths were very active in terms of EVPs and activity, which makes sense given their use.

"You think of a confessional, every evil deed or sin you've committed, or anything you might have wanted to get off your chest, you tell a priest, and God knows priests can't tell the cops. Who knows what a priest has heard over the years," says Mombourquette.

Murphy says the priest didn't have the best reputation, and could even be considered evil. He wonders who the harsh-voice being was who they caught asking for him on the EVP.

The attic also contained a shrine of sorts for two construction workers who died in accidents while restoring the church. Mombourquette says their hard hats and hammers hung on the wall, as did the names of the deceased men.

He says hung, because the church has since been torn down, the owners unable to pay for the building's upkeep.

Haunts from the Cape never had the opportunity to return for a follow-up investigation.

Cape Breton is full of allegedly haunted locations. Much like in the Old World, the supernatural is a big part of life. Mombourquette says people will renovate houses and find old leather shoes in the wall. This was a practice done to keep witches out. And coins are still placed above doorways to keep out evil spirits.

Mombourquette mentions other encounters people had at the fortress at Louisbourg. Staff and visitors have seen spectral soldiers walking the walls, crying ghosts sitting in chairs, and one tour group saw a woman kneeling in prayer in the chapel, mumbling vulgar words in both English and French.

The tour guide kept apologizing to the tourists, thinking the woman was a staff member getting too far into her role, he says.

"As they were leaving the chapel, the tour guide turned to get at her [the kneeling woman], and she was gone," says Mombourquette.

"There's so many stories from out here."

Haunts from the Cape had their own encounter with a period ghost – or so they thought at the time — during an all-nighter at the fortress. Mombourquette admits the group was tired, so tired everyone's eyes were like "two piss holes in the snow".

The team was hanging out by one of the gates and saw a man walking toward them with a lantern in hand. Mombourquette says everyone was beside themselves.

"Are we actually seeing the actual apparition of a ghost?" they asked themselves.

The man walked past, nodded at the team, and walked into the washroom. Murphy and Mombourquette sent one of the team inside to investigate. The team member returned a moment later, saying the guy was indeed real, and going to the bathroom.

Recounting the story, Murphy and Mombourquette can't help but laugh out loud.

"It turns out the guy works there, and will stay overnight during big events. We didn't even know he was there," says Mombourquette. "He shows up at five in the morning, carrying a lantern, dressed like a French soldier..."

When it comes to equipment, Haunts from the Cape use the standards many teams rely on. Digital recorders, Spirit Boxes, motion detectors, and still and video cameras, as well as infrared cameras, are put to use on most investigations.

"We don't use a whole lot," says Murphy, adding it's best to keep it simple.

"We spent a whole lot of money, and we usually show up with just recorders in our hands," says Mombourquette.

Murphy says the team often gets its best evidence using recorders, including a small, handheld vintage device that uses tapes.

"We've got some of the best EVPs with that," he says.

As for what Murphy and Mombourquette think is behind all this activity? Murphy is convinced it is residual energy left behind when people die.

Mombourquette has yet to form an opinion, but he's leaning toward the idea ghosts might be people going about their lives in a different dimension, and encounters occur at places where the veil between dimensions is thinnest.

"Or, like Jason says, it could very easily be residual energy," he says.

Either way, Haunts from the Cape will continue to investigate the paranormal – and Cape Breton's haunted heritage - for years to come, even if an answer to why doesn't present itself.

6   AMANDA QUILL

On paper, it might look like Amanda Quill is trying to take over the world of paranormal investigation... one city and region at a time.

Located in Vancouver, Canada, Quill formed Coldspotters Paranormal in 2012 and has since had chapters spring up in communities in North America, reaching across Florida and even internationally in Croatia, New Zealand, and the Netherlands.

This investigative expansion isn't part of any grand design, but rather the continuation of a life's work that – as with many who delve into this pseudoscience - stretches back some thirty years to her childhood.

Quill wasn't out investigating abandoned buildings or haunted homes at a young age, but she was reading books and learning all she could on the subject of the paranormal. Interestingly enough, it wasn't a spooky encounter that prompted her interest, although she'd one day have her share of those, but a love of ghost stories in general.

"I had a kick at a really, really young age for ghost stories. I'd go into libraries and search up any ghost story that I could find," says Quill. "I learned all the different words for ghosts, spectres and phantoms. Using the Dewey decimal system, I'd find every single story I could get."

One day, when she was still at an age when she was too young to grasp the concept, she stumbled upon a book on actual ghost hunting. Even as a small child, the concept that ghosts might actually be real, and something one could hunt down, excited her.

"These stories are true!" she remembers thinking.

It was stories about Abraham Lincoln and his ghostly encounters in the White House, and tales similar to them, that prompted Quill to want to investigate ghosts and hauntings professionally. Her first thought was to study the subject at an actual university. When none seemed to offer any actual course on the paranormal, Quill decided to do it herself.

"I just started slowly reading the books, and understanding what cold spots were and what the different kind of hauntings were, and it just blossomed from there," Quill says.

Unlike most people who get into this field of research, Quill didn't have any personal experiences as a child. Her first occurred when she was a teenager, after she'd already spent years researching the subject. She says she always expected to encounter a ghost, she just never knew when.

Quill was fourteen or fifteen and living in a group home in East Vancouver when she had her first encounter. She calls the experience overwhelming, and has difficulty explaining it to this day.

"But it was pretty cool," she says.

There were eight girls aged thirteen to sixteen living in the home at the time when the haunting, which Quill suspects was a poltergeist, began. Quill says all the girls were going through some rough times and emotional trauma, which many believe is the trigger for poltergeist activity.

Books would be tossed off shelves by invisible hands, crown moulding popped out of one-hundred-year-old ceilings, plates and cups were thrown from kitchen cupboards, and scratches appeared on walls. Quill says none of the girls were responsible for any of this, but the owners of the home placed the blame squarely on them.

At that young age, Quill didn't understand what poltergeist activity was. At the time she simply believed there were hauntings, and then there were the haunted. She's since learned otherwise, she says.

A poltergeist is a type of ghost or spirit that's responsible for physical disturbances like loud noises and objects being moved or even destroyed. At times poltergeists have been blamed for biting, pinching, hitting or even tripping people.

Poltergeist is the German word for noisy ghost or noisy spirit, and much of the activity, such as the Enfield Poltergeist case in England, or the Bell Witch haunting in the Southern United States, is centred around an adolescent, usually a girl.

Investigators don't always agree on what a poltergeist actually is. Some believe the activity is the result of a ghost or spirit, while others think it originates from "unknown energy" associated with a living person or place. Taken a step further, poltergeist events could be caused by the pent-up emotions of a troubled individual that are unconsciously projected outward as a form of mental energy, which impacts the physical environment around them.

Back to Quill's experience. At the time, she believed the activity was related to the group home she was staying in. She says the home was built in the early 1900s and had seen many tenants before becoming an orphanage and care home for wards of the province.

One day, toward the end of Quill's stay at the home, a past owner came by for a visit and tour. As the woman was leaving, she paused, looked right at Quill, and said, "He's here to protect you, just so you know."

Quill says she was taken aback by the statement, which prompted the woman to continue. "You know exactly who

I'm talking about. It's George. We used to call him George, and he's here to protect you."

So Quill assumed the haunting was George's fault, and she believed George lived in the attic, which was where a lot of the activity took place. She says windows would fly open, and panes of glass would explode. Adding to the strangeness of these experiences was the fact the door to the attic had long been sealed and a wall built across it, making it impossible for anyone to get into the attic.

Despite that fact, the owners continued to blame the girls for the destruction, she says.

"How are we the ones breaking the glass? Wouldn't the glass go in [to the home] if we were breaking the windows? We'd have to throw things at them from the outside," she says.

It wasn't until years later, after Quill had continued her research into the paranormal, that she realized George – if there was a George – had nothing to do with the destruction. She's convinced the girls, and their trauma, created the activity.

"It's an interesting thing to look back to," says Quill.

She didn't begin investigating until she was seventeen, when she met two women who investigated in and around Vancouver through the 1990s. They would take Quill on investigations that involved young families, as she could relate to them and comfort them through the activity. At the time, there weren't many groups investigating the paranormal. Quill says those didn't turn up, at least in Vancouver, until they were popularized on television.

The first group she joined was Edmonton Paranormal

in the early 2000s, when she'd relocated to Alberta. Quill had been investigating on her own as she moved continuously back and forth across Canada, but found it increasingly difficult due to the popularity of shows like *Ghost Hunters*. Every time she'd inquire about investigating a haunting, people wanted to know what group she was a part of. If she had no affiliation, she wouldn't be allowed to investigate.

Quill formed Coldspotters for just that reason when she moved back to Vancouver.

When it comes to her most memorable case – at least in terms of the most validating experiences – Quill has to stop and think about it. Each case is unique to her in its own way. But one that currently stands out is also one that's ongoing with Coldspotters to this day.

"I always find that you find the best evidence when you're able to attend a place more than one to three times," she says.

Coldspotters was called into one of the older mansions in the Lower Mainland a while ago. Typically, any investigator or team will want to research a location thoroughly before investigating, so as to get a good idea of what the activity might be.

In a rare turn, Quill and company didn't do that. They went in cold. Quill says the owners asked if the team wanted to know the backstory or not, and they wanted a challenge, so they said no.

"Challenge accepted," says Quill with a laugh.

The team visited the home three times before they sat down with the homeowners. Quill says they captured some compelling EVPs during those investigations, including a man coughing, which they caught on both audio recorders and video cameras, in an empty room.

A young girl's voice was also recorded on audio, and one of the team even convinced this spirit to recite the alphabet, says Quill.

"One of our investigators was doing the A,B,Cs, and the next letter was actually heard in the young girl's voice," she says.

On one occasion, heavy footsteps were recorded going down the main flight of stairs. Another time, they heard walking on the floor above them, she says. One compelling piece of video footage shows a person peeking out from around a corner, and a large arm swinging out as well.

When the evidence was presented to the client, every family member became quite excited when they heard the cough. "They got him! They got him!" the owners said.

"That was one of their main things, the Coughing Man," says Quill. "Apparently he was a soldier who had TB [tuberculous] and had died in that mansion."

She adds the owners could hear the Coughing Man on the stairs and upstairs if they were on the main level, which matches up with what Coldspotters was capturing with their audio and video. She says the owners also claimed they heard a little girl singing, and would see her peek out around corners at them near the stairs.

"That was kind of interesting that, in the videos, we'd get a smaller person peeking and a larger person too," says Quill.

Quill returned to the house a fourth time and did an

EVP session on her own. She was upstairs in a sun-room, and it was raining out. Quill was explaining to the room theories around rain and energy – how water is believed to be a life-giving power and a symbol for purification, protection, and healing – and if any spirits need "an extra boost in their day", they could open a window. To drive this point home, she opened a window, letting the sound and smell of rain drift in.

"I said, 'This is my favourite window,' and you could actually hear, in my recorder, the rain gets a little bit louder," she says.

The session over, she reviewed her audio for any EVPs, but didn't record anything, she says. However, she could hear herself close the window and the window latch, but the sound of the rain remained just as loud in the room as it did with the window open.

"That's something I didn't actually notice while I was doing the investigation," says Quill.

When Coldspotters returned again, the owners told the team they had new activity going on at the mansion. Whenever it would rain, neighbours and passersby would tell them the upstairs windows would be open!

Quill wonders now if she should have asked the spirits to close the windows when they were done gathering that extra energy...

She believes this is proof that spirits and people can communicate and interact with each other on some level.

"Maybe what they're doing is sticking around, and we're looking for it, but maybe what we're doing is sticking around too," she says.

While this investigation provided her with the most validating evidence, Quill's most engaging personal experience occurred elsewhere. It happened not during a case, but at a home she lived in at the time, and the encounter was the first time she saw an apparition.

Quill had often wondered how she would react if she actually saw a ghost with her own eyes. She contemplated if the situation would be a be-careful-what-you-wish-for scenario? Would she freak out and run screaming from the room? Or would she react nonchalantly and simply walk away bored.

"I was calm," she said of the actual experience. "It kind of solidified for me that this isn't about seeing a ghost or proving that they're real. It's figuring out what this [the paranormal] is adding to maybe my life, or maybe adding to other people's lives. Maybe it's about how I can help anyone's journey, or how I can help my own."

Seeing an apparition made it clear in Quill's mind that her career as a paranormal investigator isn't born of some obsession with the dead, it's more of an obsession with life and helping others understand how precious it is, she says.

This belief forms the core of what Quill thinks the paranormal is. She believes it's a natural part of life and the world around us and a means to help us navigate our lives and the world around us. If it is a way of aiding us on our journey to the other side, which she thinks it is, Quill doesn't believe we'll know all the facts until we get there.

But she doesn't think we should be too focused on what happens after we die, but instead remain planted firmly in the life we're living now, she says. That's the most important lesson the paranormal can teach us.

"It's definitely part of my journey and who I am, in my culture, and in my spirit. I believe this is what I'm supposed to do," she says. "And if I'm not scared of sitting in the dark and asking the walls questions, then that's what I should do."

7   SCOTT MOON

Paranormal investigators come from all walks of life. During our time in the field, Peter and I have met ghost hunters whose day jobs include clinical psychologists, construction workers, care aids, photographers, and even engineers.

When Scott Moon started investigating ghosts, he was an ordained minister. Given how many religions view the paranormal, seeing it as a tool of the devil, this might come as a surprise. But he saw an opportunity to investigate alleged hauntings as a way to help him understand the field he was in at the time, as a man of the church.

It was also these opportunities to investigate alleged paranormal activity that soon prompted him to leave the church and focus his life on the pursuit of the supernatural.

Moon won't provide the name of the church he belonged to, but says the hierarchy was very much against him pursuing the paranormal as an extracurricular activity.

"They were extremely against it. They wanted to pull my ordination at first," says Moon.

He argued that in the Bible Jesus hung out with murderers and tax collectors and spread the gospel that way. How was what he was doing any different? That didn't sit well with his higher-ups, he says.

"What I'm called to do has nothing to do with what's in [the Bible]. It has nothing to do with people's opinions. It has everything to do with God himself," he says. "I'm not going to satisfy people doing this. It's not going to happen. So I separated from the church."

He acknowledges this was a dramatic shift in his life, but one he doesn't regret. Moon does, however, bring much of what he learned during his time as an ordained minister into his investigative work with Meagun Humphries and her Panhandle Paranormal Investigations, which he joined nine years ago in Florida. This includes a firm belief in the demonic and its influence on the world around us.

"They are a very big network. I think they exist a lot more prevalently than we think," Moon says of demons.

Any negative influences in our lives are likely the result of demons, who Moon says are deceitful liars. He likens them to the negative self-talk we have due to societal pressures about body image and personal success. In fact, demons will feed on and encourage such activity.

"I think they're everywhere. I think they're a big network. And if one sees you, they all see you," says Moon. "It's kinda like Facebook; you like a picture and then it goes viral. It's that kind of thing."

In religious circles, demons are believed to be fallen angels who followed Lucifer to Hell after God kicked him out of Heaven. Those who believe in demons feel their very existence is to tempt people into immoral acts and drive a wedge between humans and God.

The term demon is derived from the Greek word daimon, meaning divine power or god. The actual translation means "replete with wisdom", suggesting demons are knowledgeable creatures, which is evident in their knowledge of an individual's sins.

In modern times, demons are associated with evil. But in pre-Christian and non-Christian cultures, they aren't necessarily good or evil. This might seem confusing given how demons are portrayed in popular culture, especially in films like *The Exorcist* or *The Conjuring*. Regardless, when it comes to demonic possession, demonologists – those who make a practice of studying demons – believe even possession by a non-evil demon requires an exorcism.

Many paranormal investigators, at least those outside of the television circuit, are hesitant to consider demons as the cause of alleged hauntings or strange behaviours related to them. Given Moon's background, it should come as no surprise that he believes demons play a part in a small percentage of cases he's investigated. When asked, he says about twenty-five percent of the investigations he's been on have had some form of demonic influence.

He's not saying these cases have been severe, with people possessed or crosses spinning off the walls, but there's definitely something not right about the situation.

"You notice that, whenever you bring up sacred things, religious things, sacred objects, that there's an actual reaction to that," says Moon. "Not like 'Oh, look, it's going to catch on fire and burn', or 'Oh, this person is going to start throwing up green puke'. You notice the temperature in the room changes, and you get this heavy feeling."

People's behaviour also makes Moon wonder if a demonic presence is influencing the situation. Moon is convinced some of the cases he and Panhandle Paranormal have been on have definitely been influenced in such a way.

"I'm not saying everything is a demon, because it's not. It's completely not. But if you look at what demons are, what do they feed off of? Aggression? If you're very aggressive, do they come around you? I don't know. They could," he says.

"But if you call me for paranormal things, and you're beating your children? One, I'm going to call social services. Then we have to look at what's causing this. You were good one day, the next day you had a family member die, and then you threw your Bible in a trash can and started cussing everybody out and hitting them. And now you're claiming that things are flying across your house. We gotta stop and think about this."

At this point, Moon needs to consider all options, he says. And yes, consulting a doctor and psychologist are among those considerations.

"Most of the times, it's a doctor," says Moon. "But maybe twenty-five percent of the time, with the cases I've been on, it's been something not normal. This isn't a poltergeist or your run-of-the-mill 'I'm scared'. This isn't like 'Okay, we've got a shadow person'."

Panhandle Paranormal developed a method to help suss out any potential demonic activity. Moon says he will take a Saint Michael pendant and toss it somewhere in the home or on the property where he is confident one of the people involved will pick it up. If they pick it up and present it to him while physically touching it, then he's sure the demonic isn't at work.

If someone doesn't want to touch the Saint Michael pendant, and even reacts in fear to it, then Moon suspects something is up, he says.

Given their evil – unholy even – nature, demons are unable to touch holy objects. A pendant or image of Saint Michael is especially potent because, according to Catholic teachings, he was the enemy of Satan and responsible for sending Satan and his fallen angels to Hell.

Moon insists his approach is a personal take on the subject of demons. Another investigator or priest will look at things differently.

"I just notice, whenever we go places, we take a baseline of a person's behaviour. And, if that baseline changes, that's when you ask 'What's causing it to change?'" says Moon.

Of those twenty-five percent of cases, Moon has one that stands out as particularly strange and unsettling. Panhandle Paranormal was summoned to a home in a poor residential neighbourhood by a couple who were experiencing activity. Given the nature of the neighbourhood, Moon immediately suspected drug use might be involved.

However, the husband was from Mexico and very big into Nuestra Senora de la Santa Muerte, a cult image and folk saint in Mexican neopaganism and folk Catholicism, says Moon. A personification of death, she is associated with healing, protectionism, and safe passage to the afterlife.

The cult of Santa Muerte began in Mexico in the mid-twentieth century and remained under the radar until the 1990s, with rituals, prayers and other rites generally performed in people's homes. The cult has now become more public, and membership has grown to upwards of twenty million people in Mexico, the United States, and parts of Central America.

Moon and company didn't know this going in, but they started experiencing activity almost as soon as they arrived at the home, he says. They saw shadow people moving about the house with great frequency, and more than one member of the team would see them at any given time.

When the team first arrived, the wife seemed ignorant to concepts of religion and the paranormal, says Moon. She also appeared to be high on some kind of drug. The couple left their home to allow the team to investigate, and when they returned, her demeanor was completely different.

"She went from being erratic to being very proper and knowledgeable about verses in the Bible and what they meant," he says. "It didn't seem like the same person."

Panhandle Paranormal returned to the home for two follow-up investigations. Moon brought several investigators with him for the second investigation and experienced nothing. But when they returned for a third time and only brought three or four members with them, the home was just as active as the first time.

And, almost as soon as they arrived that third time, everyone on the team had the distinct feeling they were not welcome. There were horrible, sulphuric smells and disturbing sounds. The shadow beings were once again present, and there was a general sense of oppression in the home.

"It was very disorienting," says Moon. "The entities in the place were very guarded against us being in the place. They were very territorial. That's the only way I can describe it. I don't know how to describe it. I've never come across it again."

The wife's behaviour was also erratic and reminiscent of Moon's first visit. Although not an expert, Moon believes she at least displayed symptoms of demonic oppression.

Depending on what you read or where you research, the signs of demonic oppression and possession can vary. But it's generally agreed upon by those who believe in such things that those under the influence display a shift in personality, not unlike what Moon and company experienced with the wife. Sometimes the possessed/oppressed person has spoken in a voice different from his or her own, and displayed an almost supernatural knowledge of things they wouldn't normally know about, which also correlates to what Moon experienced.

Increased strength and other heightened abilities have also been associated with cases of alleged demonic possession and oppression.

It should also be noted that many of these symptoms can also be attributed to mental illness, especially schizophrenia, and have also been seen in people under the influence of certain drugs.

In the end, Moon referred the wife to the local Catholic church for follow-up.

When it comes to the equipment Moon uses, he prefers to use ones he creates himself. Yes, Moon is an inventor of sorts who likes to think outside the box when it comes to the tools he brings to the trade.

Moon has replicated the REM pod, which is a small, compact device that radiates an electromagnetic field. It's equipped with an antenna that detects disturbances in the area around it in 360 degrees. The invention uses sound and coloured lights to warn a paranormal investigator of unseen movement.

"There's surprisingly nothing to it," he says.

He's also made his own laser microphones, which use a laser device to detect sound vibrations in distant objects, receivers and transmitters, and radar motion sensors that work with a Doppler effect, which means it detects sound-wave motion between a wave source and the device.

Moon has also built "laser trips", which work like the old-fashioned string with a bell stretched across a doorway. In this case, anything breaks the laser beam and the trip goes off.

"I've got so many I don't even know where to start," he says, adding he's created more motion sensors than he can keep track of. "It's basic stuff for our field."

Like most investigators, Moon likes to do his research before going in, and hear the claims of those experiencing alleged activity. He then tries to rule out any natural expla-nation before he and his team investigate. Once they proceed, Moon determines the best places to set up equip-ment in hope of capturing any evidence for the client.

"And then we set up outside of where most of these issues are occurring, so we can hear what's going on there as well," he says. "Most of the time it's a possum. Most of the time, we're trying to debunk as much as we can."

What prompted his foray into the paranormal to begin with, long before he first went investigating with friends? Like almost everyone in this field, Moon had a personal experience when he was young. His occurred when he was twelve, after the death of a family member.

Moon says he was in his room and in mourning. He kept saying aloud, "I can't believe you're gone, I can't believe you're gone."

Then, for whatever reason, he said: "If you're still around, please let me know."

As if on cue, his radio turned on, and it was cranked full volume to a local station.

"And it was one of those old radios where you had to push the button to turn it on, and it had the record player on top and tapes and stuff," he says. "It scared the shit out of me."

The young Moon was so startled by this he ran from the room.

He also spent part of his youth growing up in Puerto Rico, which is one of the more haunted places in the Caribbean. Yet despite the area's reputation, he never experienced one incident of paranormal activity.

"Those two incidents kind of made me go, 'I wonder.' Because one was supposed to be haunted, and I experienced nothing," he says.

And what does he think of all the activity he's seen, especially given his background with the church? Moon is of two minds about it all. On the one hand, he believes he and other paranormal investigators are encountering actual people from our world who have passed on, and the demonic entities they sometimes cross paths with are the "guards at the door", as he calls them.

"Or the possible weird feelings we get when we go by a cemetery, because that's what's guarding it," he says.

But he's not willing to rule out the possibility of a

multiverse, which is gaining steam among quantum scientists and some in the paranormal field. This theorizes that ghosts, cryptids, UFOs and the like are beings from a different universe that operates parallel to ours. We're able to interact with them, and they with us, at places and points in time when the veil between dimensions is thinnest.

"There's not much I know [about this] because I'm not dead yet," he says, and laughs.

The multiverse angle intrigues him most, and he believes it could explain the existence of Sasquatch and unidentified flying objects, says Moon.

Whatever the origin, Moon and Panhandle Paranormal will continue to investigate as best they can, and hope a definitive answer will one day present itself.

8 SETH BREEDLOVE

Almost every paranormal investigator, researcher and enthusiast has an origin story that inspired him or her to embark on their quest into the unknown. It's usually a scare or an unexplainable encounter that prompts the question: what's out there?

Not so for filmmaker and documentarian Seth Breedlove. His journey into the paranormal was strictly out of boredom.

"My origin story for the paranormal blows," says Breedlove. "I don't have any crazy abduction experience or anything that got me into this stuff."

Breedlove, who comes from a newspaper background, once found himself working at a medical billing company. The job afforded him a lot of time to listen to podcasts or sit and read if he wanted to. For whatever reason, the boredom that came with the job prompted him to listen to shows about, and read books on, the paranormal.

The case of the Minerva Monster was one of the stories he explored during his time at the medical billing company, and it struck a chord with Breedlove because the incident took place near his hometown in Ohio.

In 1978, a Minerva, Ohio, family garnered national attention when they reported numerous sightings of a hairy, upright creature stalking the grounds around their home. This prompted investigations by police and Bigfoot researchers alike.

"I'd always known about that case, but because of learning more about it because of podcasts and stuff, and reading about it online, I started investigating it for myself," says Breedlove. "That was like the gateway into all of this for me."

Breedlove is the founder of Small Town Monsters, a documentary film company that focuses on small-town folklore. Breedlove writes, produces, and directs his films with the aid of his wife, Adrienne, and a dedicated team of filmmakers. His films get to the heart of the myths and legends they document by connecting with those who were most affected by them – the witnesses and small-town residents.

Minerva Monster was Breedlove's first film, and it was released in 2015. Small Town Monsters has since gone on to release ten feature-length documentaries detailing such renowned cases as the Mothman, the Bell Witch, the Boggy Creek Monster and more.

Small Town Monsters has also produced a number of series under the On the Trail of banner, including *On the Trail of Bigfoot, On the Trail of Champ* – which investigates the Lake Champlain monster – and *On the Trail of UFOs* featuring Into the Fray podcast host and Beyond the Fray Publishing co-founder, Shannon LeGro.

Making it in the film industry is tough, be it the Hollywood or independent route. Money is tight, if not nonexistent, and filmmakers often hold down full-time jobs – if not two – and film on evenings and weekends. Even once a film is shot and edited, there can be a fight to find distribution and turn a profit.

"Actually getting our first movie going was simple enough. It's easy enough to grab some cameras and go out and make a movie. But it's not easy to sustain a business for years at a time," says Breedlove.

Indeed, once Breedlove and Adrienne decided to make Small Town Monsters their life's work as a sustainable, family-run business, they found it a challenge to stay afloat for the first couple of years. Breedlove worked a part-time job during Small Town Monsters' initial two years while his wife continued to work full time. And Breedlove's crew worked for free during that time.

"Really, my wife and I were also unpaid," Breedlove says, and laughs.

Minerva Monster was in preproduction in 2014. Breedlove says Small Town Monsters finally started to sustain itself as a money-making venture by 2017, which was when Breedlove and Adrienne were able to focus on the company full time.

"Now the hardest part is just keeping it alive year to year. It hasn't gotten any easier, and when you're fighting an uphill battle against megacorporations who want to cut payouts to independent creators on a daily basis, that alone will challenge you," he says.

At the end of the day, filming movies about monsters is the easiest part of what Small Town Monsters does. The filming and editing are the fun parts of the job. Breedlove says keeping everyone on the crew happy, promoting what they're doing, and keeping the company afloat while competing with billion-dollar networks are the hard parts of the job.

Oh, and the Breedloves also became parents during the time they got Small Town Monsters off the ground, which posed its own challenge on top of everything else, he says.

Breedlove is often asked by other independent film-makers how they can get a similar production company off the ground. He says there is no one-size-fits-all answer, because every project and filmmaker is unique.

"It was timing and luck that led to where we are. It's not like we had some secret to filmmaking, or secret to how we approach the paranormal. No one else was doing what we were doing when we started in 2015," says Breedlove.

Amazon Prime was one of the first streaming services to feature Small Town Monsters' work. Back then, the paranormal content on the site was practically nonexistent. *Minerva Monster* and Breedlove's follow-up, *Beast of Whitehall*, were the first documentaries of their kind to appear on Amazon, which made Small Town Monsters a trailblazer for the genre.

Now, paranormal content is a dime a dozen on streaming services and YouTube. What makes Small Town Monsters stand out from the majority is the quality of Breedlove and his team's work. A Small Town Monsters production, be it a feature film or series, mixes interviews, on-location shooting, research and dramatic recreations – often animated – into a compelling and linear story. With the majority of other paranormal productions, that is not the case.

"Budgets don't matter; how much money you have doesn't matter. At the end of the day, it just comes down to doing something that looks like you are at least trying, and takes some sort of approach to the stuff that does what it can to set it apart from what's on the networks," says Breedlove.

"I see a lot of independent filmmakers who kind of forget the quality part. They'll just throw together something and clearly make no attempt to really try to make something of high quality."

Breedlove believes it's also a mistake to try to produce an independent version of what's on television. He says grabbing a random cryptozoologist, putting him or her in front of the camera, and trying to duplicate what Josh

Gates of *Destination Truth* and *Expedition Unknown* does won't work either.

"But people do these things, and that's mostly what you see on Amazon," he says.

When it comes to pioneers in the independent paranormal documentary world, Breedlove has his favourites and believes they are filmmakers anyone interested in documenting this phenomenon should watch. He cites Sean Whitley, who wrote and directed 2007s *Southern Fried Bigfoot*, *Eyes of the Mothman* director Matthew J. Pellowski, and J. Michael Long as inspirations for himself and anyone else with an interest in the subject matter.

"I saw *Eyes of the Mothman* the year it came out, which I think was in 2011, and I thought it was a very well-done documentary," says Breedlove.

Paranormal documentaries aren't Breedlove's only inspirations. He's a fan of film in general and credits his mom with helping him develop an interest in movies. She exposed him to the works of Ray Harryhausen, who was a pioneer in special effects thanks to his work on movies like *The Seventh Voyage of Sinbad* and *Jason and the Argonauts*. He also grew up enjoying the original *King Kong*, the Marx Brothers, and other classic films.

In fact, Breedlove believes the absurdist humour of the Marx Brothers – an American family comedy act that entertained audiences on Broadway and in feature films from 1905 to 1949 – has made its way into Small Town Monsters' first original web series, *On the Trail of Hauntings*, despite him not directing the episodes.

But the biggest influence on Small Town Monsters

and the work Breedlove creates is the long-running NBC reality series *Unsolved Mysteries*, which broadcast for fifteen seasons starting in 1987. Hosted by actor Robert Stack, the show used re-enactments and interviews to retell the circumstances surrounding mysteries that have gone unsolved. Episodes often dipped into the paranormal, tackling lake monsters and other unexplained events.

"I hated that show as a kid. My grandmother would watch it, and it absolutely terrified me," says Breedlove.

"I still find myself trying to impart some of that *Unsolved Mysteries* vibe into our films. That's the only influence that is conscious, where I'm still looking back at what they did with *Unsolved Mysteries* and trying to put that into what we do."

There are also times where Breedlove is stylistically harkening back to a genre or period of filmmaking. He tried to capture the vibe of a 1950s B-movie in *The Flatwoods Monster*, and parts of *The Bray Road Beast* harken back to the classic Hammer horror films, says Breedlove.

Fans who have watched *MOMO: The Missouri Monster* might notice the re-enactments have a 1970s drive-in movie vibe to them as well.

"There's a lot of film influence, but I don't think I'm consciously drawing off of it," he says.

Every filmmaker develops a style of his or her own. But Breedlove doesn't believe he has one yet, and instead lets the subject matter dictate his approach to it, as he did with the aforementioned films. He cites an interview with Steven Spielberg around the time the legendary director made *Jaws*, where Spielberg said it takes many years and many films for a director to develop one.

"I wouldn't know what my style is at all despite the fact I've made so many projects," he says.

In fact, Breedlove doesn't even watch a lot of new movies. Instead, he reads and watches interviews with various directors to find his inspiration. And he doesn't mean in terms of tone or style, but simply to give him the kick in the butt he needs to go out and make a film. He says reading about making movies gets him excited to run out into the woods with his friends and make a movie.

Of all the film shoots Breedlove has been on, and all the small towns he's visited in search of evidence of monsters and ghosts, he's had very few experiences that have convinced him there's any truth to the stories he's been documenting.

One of those incidents occurred in southeast Oklahoma while Breedlove was shooting *On the Trail of Bigfoot*. He was on private property in the middle of nowhere with a group of Bigfoot researchers and was lying in a bunk at night, trying to sleep.

Out of the dark, something threw a rock at the bunkhouse and let out a scream, he says. He didn't see what it was, and no cameras were rolling. But Breedlove had spent the day looking for Bigfoot, in an area where the creature was believed to be active.

"That's my only experience, as far as cryptid or paranormal related. That's the only thing that's happened to me. And that was an incident that moved me from being borderline, all-the-way skeptic... to pretty sure that Bigfoot is out there," he says.

His experience making *On the Trail of Hauntings* has provided little evidence of ghostly activity as well. Breedlove was three episodes into shooting the series when we spoke, and so far has found nothing that's moved him into being a believer in the supernatural.

At one location, the team heard footsteps walking across the floor above them when there was no one on that level of the building, he says. The footsteps are audible in the actual episode. Cameras also caught what Breedlove can only describe as "ghost lights" moving through a cemetery.

The third episode was filmed at Mansfield Reformatory, a historic prison in Ohio. Like many such facilities, it comes with a long history of ghosts and hauntings, thanks to the many deaths that occurred there during the ninety-four years it was in operation, many as a result of disease, influenza and tuberculosis.

It was also the location used for the classic Morgan Freeman film *The Shawshank Redemption*.

The Small Town Monsters team spent the better part of a day at the reformatory, and while many people at the location had weird experiences, nothing directly happened to Breedlove or his crew, he says.

"And everyone told me to be really careful when we were making *The Mark of the Bell Witch*," Breedlove says of his 2020 documentary on the Bell Witch haunting. "And we did the absolute wrong things you should do when in a place supposedly haunted by the Bell Witch."

One of the historians Breedlove recruited to help tell the Bell Witch tale gave a member of the crew a piece of flint from the Bell family cabin. The crew member ended up bringing it home with him, which is considered a big no-no when trying to avoid the wrath of a vengeful spirit. Yet the Small Town Monsters team experienced no paranormal activity.

"So even the Bell Witch is kinda like leaving us alone," says Breedlove. "I think we must be the most boring paranormal investigators. Nothing cares about us. No cryptids. No interdimensional beings."

For the uninitiated, the legend of the Bell Witch, also known as the Bell Witch Haunting, stems from Southern United States folklore. The Bell Witch is a spirit who tormented the Tennessee home of John Bell in 1804, with much of the spirit's wrath directed at Bell's daughter, Elizabeth. The spirit was eventually credited with causing John Bell's death.

All this is believed to be the result of a business deal gone wrong between Bell and a neighbour, Kate Batts, who cursed the Bell family. The spirit became known as Kate and is believed to still haunt the area today.

So why does Breedlove think he's had a hard time capturing paranormal and cryptid activity on film, if such things do exist? Breedlove maintains he's there more to document than to actually investigate, and he's doing his best to keep it simple.

Most of the people you see on paranormal reality television investigate using a lot of "scientifically questionable" equipment, he says. With his documentaries, and especially with the investigating the team does in *On the Trail of Hauntings*, they bring their cameras and that's pretty much it.

"If we can, we'll try to communicate with whatever is there. But, for the most part, we're just there to make something. We don't go in with EMF readers and Spirit Boxes. We're just not going to do it," he says.

"We go in with Subway sandwiches and be ourselves, and if I were a ghost, I'd want to mess with me."

If the phenomenon is real, one shouldn't need a bunch of fancy equipment to experience it. It should just happen, says Breedlove. He reflects on that night in Oklahoma as evidence – or as close as he's found to evidence – of that.

"I didn't have my camera on, that was the first time I didn't have my camera on in southeast Oklahoma, because I was asleep. And so that's when something happens."

Despite the lack of on-camera evidence Breedlove has captured so far, or perhaps because of it, he will continue to travel to small towns around America and tell the folk stories that have kept people awake for hundreds of years. And, if he happens to catch evidence of any of its existence on film, that'll be good too.

9 PAUL DRAKE

British paranormal investigator Paul Drake's lifelong fascination with ghosts and other high strangeness began with a simple photograph featuring an otherworldly canine.

The year was 1988, and Drake was in his twenties when he saw the photograph in a news magazine. The picture was taken at the Dambusters Memorial in Woodhall Spar, England.

The photo shows a group of people posing in front of the memorial. In May, 1943, aircraft from the 617 squadron of the Royal Air Force attacked and destroyed two large dams in the Ruhr Valley of Germany. This was done using the now famous "bouncing bomb" developed by Barnes Wallis. The aircraft and pilots of that successful mission were dubbed the Dambusters.

A dog is visible among the group, but, according to the photographer, the dog wasn't there when the picture was taken.

"I'd seen an apparition before then, but that picture really started me onto this field that I do now," says Drake, adding to see a spirit captured on film fascinated him.

And what of the apparition Drake saw prior to the paranormal pooch? One of Drake's jobs was to deliver gaming machines to pubs. One morning, at about 8:30, he stopped at the Cornhill Vaults Pub in his hometown of Lincoln. The pub was indeed a vault, having been constructed in old subterranean tunnels beneath a grain store.

This was in the days before twenty-four-hour drinking was allowed in the United Kingdom, so there were no patrons in the building when Drake was let in. He remembers setting up the machine, then going to get his paperwork signed by the staff member on duty. Sitting at one of the tables was a man who, to Drake, seemed out of place or out of character, he says.

"He had long, black, scraggly hair to his shoulders, and his shirt was a cravat. That's quite a large collar," he says. Research would later reveal the man's appearance was in line with fourteenth or fifteenth-century attire of the area.

Drake tracked down the landlord and got his paper-work signed. Then brought up the man who was drinking in the bar.

"What man?" the landlord asked.

So Drake turned and looked around the pub. No one was there!

According to the landlord, Drake had seen an apparition other patrons had reported seeing. At first, he thought his mind was playing tricks on him, says Drake. Then he sat in his van for a minute or two, and it clicked over in his mind – he'd seen a ghost.

The encounter, as well as the Dambusters photograph, slipped into history for Drake, who busied himself with work and the demands life puts on one. It wasn't until he saw the Woodhall Spar picture again in 2001 that he decided to investigate the paranormal with great help from Michelle Clements and the continued support of all his team's members.

"That sort of all brought it back together again," he says. "I created the team and have been investigating ever since."

The team is Paranormal Links, and Drake and his colleagues have been investigating throughout England for the better part of two decades. He says forming the team wasn't easy, as many of his friends weren't interested in the paranormal at all. He placed ads in newspapers and took to online forums to make connections with like-minded people. Things slowly came together from there.

Pre-pandemic, Paranormal Links would conduct about an investigation a month, says Drake. They don't shy away from residential homes, commercial buildings, or even military bases and historic sites.

"Basically anywhere that will have us," he says.

He finds homeowners are the most unique of his clientele given they're willing to let complete strangers into their homes. Drake can't think of any other hobby, for lack of a better word, where people do that.

Then again, given the nature of what people are experiencing in their homes, and the stigma that comes with it, he believes people are willing to let strangers in if they can help, says Drake.

Paranormal Links have conducted some two hundred investigations during two decades of service. Drake says about ten would be considered active, in that activity was documented and evidence gathered. He admits that's a small number.

"It's not like you see on TV where every location is active. That's certainly not the case," he says.

When pressed to describe a favourite case or experience, Drake is hesitant. He says every one is unique and of interest. But he has had some experiences that stand out a bit from the others. One, interestingly enough, is related to the Dambusters.

The team was allowed in to RAF Scampton in Lincolnshire, which is an active air force base complete with heritage centre and museum. Exhibits include the two Dambuster raids. Drake and his team conducted four investigations there, and says the history alone blew his mind.

"The historical side alone really grabbed me," he says.

How does one obtain access to a military base like this? Email! Drake says he simply emailed the base commander, explained what he and Paranormal Links wanted to do, and was pleasantly surprised when a response said come on in.

It helped that personnel on the base had seen phantom airmen from the Second World War, including some that appeared to be on fire, says Drake.

Paranormal encounters and war go hand in hand, which shouldn't be a surprise given the amount of trauma combatants and other military personnel experience. This energy has to go somewhere, and some believe it manifests itself as apparitions and other high strangeness. Drake believes this could be the cause of hauntings at RAF Scampton and other military bases he and Paranormal Links have investigated.

Drake cites an investigation the team did at a house near Brigg, a small town near the junction of the River Ancholme and east and west transportation routes through Lincolnshire. Brigg was also featured prominently in the Doomsday Book; a manuscript record of "the Great Survey" completed in 1066 of much of England and parts of Wales by order of King William the Conqueror. The survey's main purpose was to determine what taxes were still owed during the reign of Edward the Confessor as a means of expanding William's power and that of the church.

The huge amount of information contained in the volumes – it's actually two books, not one – led many to compare it to the Last Judgement, or Doomsday, in the Bible, when the deeds of Christians written in the Book of Life were to be placed before God in judgement.

Whether or not these biblical connotations somehow played a part in the manifestation of the paranormal at the Brigg house is unknown, and unlikely. The homeowners reported objects moving about the house on their own, and something unseen touched them and made other physical contact.

Drake says a friend of the homeowner reached out to the team and asked them to investigate.

"As soon as I walked into the house, you could feel it," he says. "I don't like to make my mind up to whether a house is haunted before I go in. I want the evidence to speak, and within five minutes of walking into that house, the evidence was speaking."

Everyone on the team was hearing voices and other sounds. At one point there were some thirty investigators on-site, and each one reported hearing something they couldn't easily explain. He even invited in other teams to see if their experiences backed up what Paranormal Links encountered.

They did.

Drake and his team were also assaulted by a presence there.

"I got scratched. A friend of mine had the scratch of what looked like a fishing hook on his hand," says Drake.

"One of the people who used to live there was a fisherman. You tie things together."

A REM pod, which investigators use to track movement, would go off with no one visibly present. This alone can be interesting and exciting. But Drake and his team soon realized there was a pattern within the pod's lights and sound.

"It was giving out Morse code," he says. "We recorded the Morse code, had a professional decode it, because I wasn't going to decode it myself. What it was giving out were letters. Now, those letters turned out to be a call sign for a Lancaster that crashed in that area."

The Avro Lancaster was a four-engine bomber the British Royal Air Force used during the latter half of World War II. A search of British aviation incident logs revealed several crashes throughout the area, some resulting in fatalities.

"This Morse code played over and over and over again. And it did tie into the history of the area," says Drake.

People reported seeing ghostly figures walking through the garden, so Paranormal Links set up an SLS camera, which can create images based on movement that isn't available to the naked eye. Drake says the technology is questionable at best, but they did capture a compelling image.

The SLS picked up the stick image of what looked like a person in the garden then it revealed the stick outline of what looked like a dog. At first, Drake thought the SLS was picking up movement from the garden's weeping willow...

then the "dog" leapt into the stick figure's arms – movement that didn't match what was going on with the tree – before it jumped up into the weeping willow.

"I'd never seen that before," he says. "It was mind bending."

Drake admits he made one crucial mistake during his investigation at the house in Brigg: he set up thirty closed circuit cameras throughout the house and had them run for the duration of the team's stay, which was twenty-four hours a day for seven days. The investigation took place in 2018, and Drake is still reviewing all the footage.

"That's a lesson for ya," he says.

The house in Brigg has since been demolished.

CCTV cameras and REM pods aren't the only tools in Paranormal Links' investigative arsenal. Drake and company come equipped with SLS cameras, digital recorders, a thermal camera, and more. As he puts it, there's enough equipment to fill a van.

"We started off with a digital camera and an EMF meter. That would go into a kit bag. Now we've got a full van," he says.

Drake admits most of the equipment doesn't get used. He and his teammates usually rely on the tried-and-true digital recorders and cameras. He acknowledges that thirty CCTV cameras equates to thirty more investigators on-site, which is great when investigating in a large building, but that can be cumbersome, as he's learned with the house at Brigg. He says all that equipment can get in the way.

Due to the technology being similar to what's used in

motion-sensitive video games, Drake is disappointed with the SLS camera. He says most of what it detects is questionable and can't be trusted, as the device will try to make sense out of any pattern it picks up. Most of the time, there's nothing paranormal in its findings.

He concedes the footage it picked up at Briggs was compelling, though. And if used in conjunction with an infrared camera that was also detecting similar activity at the same time, he'd give the SLS more weight. Otherwise, the camera isn't used all that often.

When it comes to the secrets behind the activity Drake has experienced during his twenty years in the paranormal field, he isn't sure he wants a final answer, he says.

"If I find out, then I'm done," says Drake. "It's like somebody building a house. Once you've built the house, what's the point in carrying on with it? You could go build another one, but the house you really wanted to build, you've built it."

Pressed for theories about what he and other paranormal investigators are encountering, Drake says he changes his mind from week to week. But he's leaning toward people entering another realm when they die, and that's what investigators cross paths with when investigating a haunted location.

"The amount of energy you release when you die might be enough energy to make that jump [to the other realm]," he says. "I always say to myself, the reward for living is dying, and the reward for dying is living. There's got to be a reward for what we do at one point."

Until Drake finds that final answer and receives his reward for the life he's lived, he'll continue to look for definite answers to the paranormal throughout his native England and explore his country's history while doing so.

10   ADRIAN AND TINA SCALF

For husband and wife investigating duo Adrian and Tina Scalf, their journey into the paranormal began when they moved into a haunted house.

Even then, Tina was a believer long before Adrian, who was a deacon in his church at the time.

"Tina and the kids were experiencing paranormal

activity. I was a nonbeliever and thought she was just freaking herself out," says Adrian.

Adrian admits, and Tina willingly backs him up, that he was stubborn. Believing in ghosts was not something any sane adult did. Nor did belief in the supernatural fit into his Christian stance on what happens to people when they die.

"You die, you go up, or you go down. That's it," Adrian says.

Unlike her husband, Tina considers herself a lifelong believer in the paranormal. She was the weird kid in school who was fascinated by stories about the Mothman and Loch Ness Monster. While all the other kids were checking out library books on ponies and doing book reports on "normal" things, she read and wrote about ghosts.

"Teachers were calling my parents and wanting to talk to them about their kid," she says.

When she was seventeen and visiting an old house in her hometown, she saw a face come through a closed door, look about, and then pull back through the door, says Tina. But she chalked that up to her imagination.

The next closest thing she could attribute to a para-normal encounter was she frequently smelled her grandfather's old pipe tobacco, but he'd long since passed away, she says.

It wasn't until she and Adrian moved into a house in Fort Smith, Arkansas, which they still call home, that things really came to a head. The family was still unpacking when Tina had her first experience. Adrian had gone to work.

"All the boxes were in the front room, and I was pulling them up the stairs and putting them in the rooms they belonged in," says Tina. "I came back downstairs and noticed that the room seemed dark."

She says the room was unusually dark for the time of day, but didn't know quite what to make of it. So she took another book upstairs, and when she came back down to the front room, it was back to its usual brightness.

A couple of days later, while she was puttering about the house, Tina noticed unusual shadows flitting about in places shadows shouldn't be. Soon enough, she was seeing them scurrying around, be it day or night.

"Sometimes they were small; sometimes they were big. They weren't ever shaped like anything in particular," says Tina.

Confused, and a little concerned, Tina told Adrian she thought the house was haunted. Given she'd never tried to hide her belief in the paranormal from her husband, Adrian responded more with frustration than concern.

"Is every home we live in going to be haunted?" he asked.

Adrian says his understanding at the time was hauntings are supposed to be rare, yet Tina claimed to see spirits in other houses they'd lived in.

Tina insisted she knew what she was seeing and, the more she saw them in the home, the more they looked like animals to her, she says.

The activity persisted and was most common while

Adrian was away at work. Tina began to hear sounds and voices, and even went online looking up EVPs and paranormal videos, watching and listening to them for hours, in hope of better understanding what was going on in their home. Adrian says he thought his wife was hallucinating, or at the very least working herself into a state.

Then something started to bother her, she says. Adrian worked nights, so Tina slept alone. She soon had an invisible presence poking her feet and pulling at the covers as she tried to sleep.

"The more I was here alone, the more I was seeing stuff," she says.

It got to the point where Tina had some kind of encounter to share with Adrian every day, so he decided to placate her and bring someone in to help. Adrian says he tried to seek out a paranormal investigation team and have them visit the house. But he couldn't find one that fit into his Christian view of what could possibly be going on in his home.

"I can't find anybody who doesn't look like a kook," he told her at the time.

Adrian's solution: they should start their own team... an idea Tina was initially resistant to.

"Because every time Adrian gets to do something, Adrian has fun and Tina does all the work," she says.

Adrian agrees with his wife's assessment.

From Adrian's point of view, he began to develop an open mind thanks to an encounter he and Tina had on their way home one night, only while living at a previous home in McAlester, Oklahoma.

The Scalfs' kids were teenagers then and able to stay home alone. So Adrian and Tina had gone to the movies. They drove home along the main street in McAllister and were about to pass through the primary intersection, which was well lit with a courthouse on one side and train tracks on the other.

"We saw a creature cross the road," Adrian says, matter-of-fact. "I say creature because it didn't fit into the natural realm."

Adrian's skepticism comes from a difficulty in believing in things he hasn't seen with his own eyes, which he admits is weird coming from a Christian. He hasn't seen a Bigfoot, so he doubts its existence. And, prior to that moment, he hadn't encountered anything he'd classify as a ghost.

But whatever that was he saw on that stretch of road opened his mind a bit. He and Tina watched it for about seven-seconds, although time felt like it stood still, and the encounter lasted even longer.

"When you see something that's unbelievable, seven-seconds is a long time," says Adrian.

"It came into view, in a well-lit area, crossing four lanes in front of us. It was about two feet from the ground to its shoulders, or for the bulk of the body. No tail. The forward legs were really pronounced behind its back so they almost looked like wings."

Just before it stepped out of view, it turned and looked at them, he says. The face was unlike anything he'd seen at a zoo or on nature programs on television.

At first, Tina thought it was a tailless cat, like a black

panther, she says. But then it looked at them, and she couldn't tell what it was.

"When it looked at us, it looked like it could've had a bat face. A pushed-in, almost bull-doggy, batty face," says Tina.

Adrian brought the car to a complete stop. He says he and Tina could only sit in amazement at what they'd just witnessed. They asked each other, and quickly confirmed, what they'd just seen.

"After I saw that, I realized I don't know everything," says Adrian.

"We already knew that," Tina teases him.

Reflecting back on this, Adrian thought he should take Tina's and the children's stories about a ghostly presence in the house more seriously.

Which brings us back to the house in Fort Smith. Adrian recalls a ghostly encounter that occurred one morning when he came home from work. Adrian says he had just walked in the door, and as he looked toward the kitchen, he saw what he thought was his daughter's shadow being cast from the living room.

However, as he walked into the kitchen, the shadow had changed orientation by ninety degrees from the living room, which he suddenly realized was dark, with nothing capable of creating such a shadow.

"The only light would be coming from the window behind me," he says.

As if these encounters weren't enough, Adrian had one more he considers the showstopper, he says. He was tinkering away in his basement workshop and was about to do some work on the electrical box when something caused him to look up. Standing in the doorway was a tall, slender man with a crew cut. The figure was so distinct, Adrian could even notice he wore a button-up shirt and had a crease in his pants.

Thinking a strange man had come into his home, Adrian charged forward to challenge him. The only thing was, the man was gone, and there had been no easy escape from the room.

"He just disappeared," says Adrian. "I stood there just dumbfounded for a couple of minutes until I was like, 'Oh right. You live in a haunted house'."

Adrian turned back to work on the electrical box and noticed he'd failed to turn off the power. Had he proceeded with his work a moment earlier, he could've been electrocuted. Adrian says the man appeared as if to warn him about the pending danger.

The encounters Adrian and Tina had in their home prompted them to form River Valley Paranormal Research and Investigations in 2006. They've investigated some two hundred alleged hauntings since, and from time to time, spirits have attempted to follow them home.

Interestingly enough, whatever ghost resides in their home – and the couple is convinced it's the man Adrian saw in the basement – doesn't take kindly to ghostly visitors.

"Our house goes crazy for, like, a couple of weeks," says Adrian. "It's like he's kicking them out."

Tina says it sounds like dishes are flying about and

cabinets are falling off the walls. The whole house will shake.

"He fights with whatever we bring home. It takes a while, and there's a battle in the house," she says. "And then it gets real quiet."

No one has died in the house, but Tina learned their home is built on land that had been subdivided into plots, which eventually became the neighbourhood. She says the landowner killed his wife and then committed suicide. Their guess is he could be the one who haunts their house.

"That was the only thing I could find that was tragic at all on the land," says Tina.

River Valley Paranormal takes Tina's interest in the paranormal, and Adrian's background as an X-ray tech, plus their Christian beliefs, and uses them all to help people understand what is going on in their homes. They see themselves as educators and helpers.

"We want people to be more comfortable in their homes," says Adrian.

The Scalfs believe there are demons, ghosts and angels among us. The ghosts are simply the spirits of the dead waiting for "the trumpet to blow" and signal it is time to enter Heaven, or Hell. Yet despite bringing their Christian beliefs into play, their work has put them at odds with the church.

Adrian stepped down from being a deacon, and church members went so far as to try to talk the couple out of River Valley Paranormal. It was Tina who explained they are doing God's work by helping people understand what is happening to them, and what is going on in their homes. The church now accepts this is Adrian and Tina's calling.

"That's what we're here for. If we don't fill that void, who is going to help these people?" asks Tina.

As far as Adrian and Tina are concerned, it's their duty to keep doing this work, and bring peace to those who are haunted like they are.

11 KELLY CLAIRE BERGE

When Kelly Claire Berge was ten years old, she and her sister and neighbourhood friends spent a great deal of time exploring their community of North Burnaby, British Columbia. That wasn't unusual back then, as there were no video games or internet to distract them.

Berge wasn't quite a paranormal enthusiast when she and her gang embarked one summer day and found themselves at the old Sugar Shacks – a group of abandoned farm buildings behind a marketplace.

They wove their way through the buildings until they came to one where several of the floor boards were ripped up and a mound of dirt gathered in place. Dangling from the rafters above the dirt pile was an old rope arranged in a hangman's noose.

"It was the stuff that urban legends are made of, that some of the neighbourhood kids made up," says Berge.

She and her friends spent the afternoon gathered around the dirt pile and noose, spinning ghost stories and winding up their young, active imaginations. Then they went home, and Berge eventually got ready for bed, the afternoon's stories far from her mind.

A few minutes passed, and Berge found herself wide awake, she says. She tossed and turned and looked toward her open closet, which was maybe two feet from her bed.

Between the closet and the bed was a glowing opalescent skull floating at eye level, its vacant eyes staring back at her, Berge says.

She blinked once, then again, each time hoping the skull would go away.

"But it didn't. It stayed there," she says.

A light switched on in the hallway and Berge's mother opened a linen closet across the hall from her bedroom. Berge says that was her cue to leap out of bed and flee her room.

"I never slept in that room again."

The experience stuck with her and sparked a lifelong interest in, and fascination with, the paranormal. It became a driving force in her life, prompting her to make multiple trips to the library, where she devoured every book she could find on the subject.

This was before the internet made research easier, she says. And although she was happy to gather as much knowledge as possible, Berge still wanted to do more. At the time, she didn't know she could investigate with groups, let alone on her own, and this frustrated her.

When she was fifteen, she learned Duke University in North Carolina offered courses in parapsychology. In fact, it was the only such program in North America.

"And, of course, it was too far, and I was too young, and that sort of dashed my hopes," says Berge. "It was a little intimidating for me."

So life went on. Berge had other paranormal encounters and became no stranger to the subject, amassing a wealth of information from the research she did. She grew up, started a career, and had a son. Through all this, her interest in high strangeness did not wane.

Then came a point in 2013 when Berge decided enough was enough; she had to do something more with her interest in the paranormal than just be interested in it. She joined paranormal Facebook groups from around the globe, got to know people virtually, and learned everything she could from them, including how to conduct an investigation and what tools were best when in the field.

That was how she met Peter Renn, who was president of Vancouver Paranormal Society at the time. She became an investigator with Vancouver Paranormal and purchased equipment from Renn, who also took her to her first investigation.

"I was hooked," says Berge.

The rest is, as they say, history. Berge has taken part in hundreds of investigations all over the coastal and interior regions of British Columbia and visited many haunted locations of historical significance. She is also the society's current president.

Many of the cases she's been on can't be discussed, as Vancouver Paranormal has a strict confidentiality agreement with clients. But there are few that Berge can talk about, including the first time she investigated Camp Alexandra in White Rock, British Columbia. A former children's summer camp, the location is now host to a mix of modern and historical buildings and provides social and recreational programs for the community.

It's also home to a few spirits, which Berge and company learned on their inaugural visit.

Investigators had some luck through the night, enough that Berge wasn't quite ready to leave when their time at the camp drew to a close. She asked Renn if they could return to Cabin Five for one more investigation, as team members had experienced activity there earlier. Renn agreed.

"I really wanted to get in there. I really wanted to have some kind of experience that night," says Berge.

Berge, another investigator, and the caretaker set up inside the cabin. There are three banks of bunk beds on each wall. The caretaker sat on one bank, Berge set up on the bunk across from him, and a second investigator sat on a bed beneath a window.

Once settled, Berge asked whatever spirits were present to do something to make themselves known, she says. She even prompted the spirits to take whatever energy was needed to do so from the team's devices.

"Just communicate with us," she asked them.

Time passed before the caretaker said he felt an energy shift in the cabin, says Berge. This was followed by the other investigator claiming she saw a ball of light come in under the door.

Suddenly, the bed Berge sat on erupted with activity, as if someone was beneath it and slamming their fists against the underside with force.

"I sat on the bunk bed. I wasn't scared. It was just the coolest thing ever," says Berge. "It was so powerful."

No sooner did Berge tell everyone what had happened than the pummeling happened again, and this time it was felt by the other investigator sitting beneath the window. Berge says the force was even stronger, and this time it was enough to force her off the bed.

Everyone started talking excitedly, almost distracting them from what happened next. Berge says one of the curtains by the window lifted up on its own and then folded back down. She and the caretaker managed to see this despite their excitement, and pointed at it.

"It was crazy. You don't get those kinds of experiences every day," she says.

Then, as is often the case, the activity stopped for the night.

In terms of evidence, Berge turns to another historic location in British Columbia's lower mainland: Historic Stewart Farm. Here the farmhouse, outbuildings and grounds date back to the early 1800s, and many staff and guests have reported strange encounters.

Berge has picked up many disembodied voices with her digital recorder, including a male voice asking Renn if he "cared to be murdered", she says. While Mr. Stewart was Scottish, this voice was an upper-class English accent, perhaps mocking Renn's more cockney English accent.

She has also seen what she believes is an apparition. This occurred in one of the old bunkhouses where Chinese immigrant workers used to live on the farm. Previous investigations of the bunkhouses turned up EVPs and even saw some activity with the team's motion detectors.

On this night, the third visit to the bunkhouses to be exact, Berge, some investigators, and farm staff sat around a large table, conducting an EVP session. Berge sat facing a window, and just after everyone heard a disembodied voice fill the room, she noticed a dark shadow encompass the window and move across it before disappearing completely. The shadow appeared to be wearing a hat with a brim around it.

"It was fall. There were a lot of crunchy leaves on the ground. There was no place to go. We ran outside and looked... nothing!" Berge says.

"To me, it validates that disembodied voice we heard."

The team picked up the voice on their recorders, she says. Sadly, a video camera that was aimed at the window ended up having a full SD card, and the shadow was not recorded.

Like many investigators, Berge relies on her digital recorder and a nice, tight-fitting set of headphones the most. To her, EVPs are the most compelling form of evidence a paranormal investigator can find. She does have more equipment, including a night-vision camera, but audio has proven more invaluable than video.

As for what all this activity amounts to? With her years of research, experiences and investigations, she has no doubt spirits are around us and inhabit many of the buildings she's been in. She doesn't believe we're just about the body we wear, or the Earth we're on.

"We're so much more than that. I don't know what happens on the other side. I hope there's a Heaven, but I just don't know," she says.

She thinks the spirit realm exists parallel to ours, and that's where our consciousness goes when we die, Berge says. And sometimes it can communicate with us in this realm.

One thing Berge counts on is she will continue to search for the answers to these questions as she ventures out into haunted locations across British Columbia. And one day, she hopes she will find them.

12 CATHY ROGERS

In this day and age, if someone experiences strange goings-on in their home, or believes they have an unwanted, spectral guest staying with them, they can seek out help in the form of a paranormal investigator or psychic medium.

Unfortunately for Cathy Rogers, this wasn't the case when she and her young daughters realized the house they called home was haunted.

This was back in 2003, shortly before the concept of

paranormal investigators took off thanks to popular television shows like *Ghost Hunters*. For many, it might be hard to imagine a time when ghost-hunting groups weren't a dime a dozen and easily accessed by a Google search. Ditto the case for psychic help.

All Rogers and her daughters had at their disposal were popular horror movies like *Poltergeist*, which, she admits today, wasn't much help at the time, especially when the spooky activity got so bad it drove the three women to sleep safely together in one room.

"My one daughter had gone into her room, and she was just little at the time, I think she was four, and she came running out. She was pure white. She was just shaking," says Rogers, many years later.

"And she was like 'There's a little girl jumping on my bed'. She was shaking. She was just shaking."

Adding to the creep factor is much of the activity at the home was related to Barbie dolls, which Rogers's daughters played with all the time. The girls would put the dolls down in one room, and when the girls returned to that room, the dolls would have moved with no explanation as to how.

One of the girls received a new Barbie doll for her birthday. As she opened it, the family dog – who was usually quite docile – suddenly changed its demeanour.

"You could literally see its eyes change. We had to keep him chained up. We couldn't let him near my daughter," says Rogers.

The dog became so vicious Rogers eventually had to

take it to the SPCA so it could be adopted out to another family, she says.

"It was like whatever was in that house associated with that Barbie doll. And the dog associated whatever it was with my daughter, because it was so instant," says Rogers.

The family's solution? They sold the house and moved into the one Rogers currently calls home. Not long after, her son was born.

At a year to a year and a half, the boy had a knack for seeing things no one else could. Rogers says he repeatedly described seeing "a guy" in the house. The boy would play with him and even have whole conversations with him.

Even her son's teacher noticed the boy's... talents. Rogers discovered her son was telling people things about them he'd otherwise not be privy to, and saw things no one else could see. There was even an incident on the school playground where the boy kept talking about a kid with a needle near the slide. She says her son refused to play there because of the kid with the needle.

This fear of the slide and whatever unseen presence was there lasted two weeks, says Rogers. Then her son told her it was okay for him to play there again.

"The little boy told me he's not going to hurt me, so I'm going to be okay," Rogers's son told her.

The teacher, dumbfounded by the boy's story, did some research and learned a sixteen-year-old boy had died from a drug overdose near the playground's slide, says Rogers. This was who her son had been seeing.

Rogers has had similar experiences herself, but was so focused on raising her children she didn't pay them much attention. But the incident with her son on the playground changed that and piqued her interest in the paranormal.

"I just always seemed to know things, very much like my children, but you always just dismiss it as an adult," says Rogers.

Rogers considers herself a medium, meaning she's a person through whom the dead are allegedly able to communicate to the living, and a practicing one. She doesn't allow just any spirit to speak through her, she says. But if she's giving a client a reading and a dead relative does approach, Rogers will connect the two.

Her time and talents aren't only spent giving people insights into the future, or providing advice for their love life. Rogers is also an investigator with Edmonton Paranormal Society and has been using her abilities to aid the team since 2009.

"When things come to me, I will absolutely bring it up or discuss it with the team, or look into it a lot deeper," she says.

That being said, Rogers still keeps herself pretty closed off, she says. She doesn't want to be the person who walks around saying, "I see dead people."

"I've got my own life," she says.

In terms of her psychic abilities, Rogers doesn't believe it's a coincidence she and her children share similar talents. Her oldest daughter and her son seem more in tune with the paranormal world around them, she says. Her younger daughter is quite intuitive, but is less interested in engaging in her talents.

Her son has a knack for predicting deaths, especially

among celebrities. The first time she recognized this was back in 2016, says Rogers. Her son came downstairs one morning and told her he had this strange urge to listen to music by Prince, but didn't know why. This wasn't a musician he normally listened to. Rogers didn't know how to answer that, but said go ahead.

The next day, April 21, 2016, Prince died.

Her boy's abilities struck again recently when he decided, for reasons he couldn't explain, he needed to watch *Black Panther*, the Marvel blockbuster starring Chadwick Boseman, who died of cancer on August 28, 2020.

"He's not a movie person. He's a YouTuber and gamer," she says, adding her son did watch *Black Panther* that night.

"The next day, Chadwick died."

His list of celebrity death predictions goes on and on and encompasses everyone from rap stars to Prince Phillip, says Rogers. Some might find this ability kooky or even gruesome, but Rogers sees it as a natural extension of his psychic abilities, which is shared within her family.

With herself, Rogers didn't realize her ability to see the dead was different or strange until she realized not everyone was able to do it. Nor did she think it weird she could predict who was phoning the family home without answering the phone almost every time a call came in. And this was prior to call display.

"I couldn't understand why everybody else didn't know who was on the phone, because to me it was so clear," she says. "This is who is on the phone! Can you not hear it?"

Once she realized her abilities weren't the norm, she became quite good at muting it, as Rogers calls it. She stopped talking about what she was seeing and feeling with others until she decided to make the paranormal her life's calling.

After she began performing readings and investigating alleged hauntings, Rogers started sharing her gift with others again. To her surprise, people mostly embraced what she could do, and told her it was no surprise she chose mediumship and paranormal investigations to express it.

She even learned after the fact that her girlfriends brought potential boyfriends to meet her, and if she didn't react strangely to them, the girls would go on to date them, she says.

As for who Rogers inherited the talent from, she's unsure, as she was adopted. She has started to track down any birth family and has come in contact with her biological brother, who lives in Quebec. Interestingly enough, he too works in the spiritual field.

As well, Rogers's adopted mom is also quite intuitive, which helped growing up, she says. If Rogers talked about any of the spiritual things she was feeling or seeing, her mother believed her.

"We were also raised quite Catholic, so it wasn't something we really talked about. It was just 'What's your intuition on this? Okay, I trust that'. And then you move on," she says. "But none of it was discussed in the realm of the paranormal."

Speaking of the paranormal, Rogers enjoys mixing her talents with the more scientific – or as some would say pseudo-scientific – way of being an investigator. She applied both to many investigations during the last twelve years, but a two-day investigation in Slave Lake definitely sticks out in her mind.

Slave Lake is a small, northern Canadian town almost two hundred miles north of Edmonton. The community was formed during the early fur trade in Canada and developed around several trading posts back in the early 1800s.

The town was ravaged by several forest fires in 2011, which forced all of the more than six thousand residents to flee for their lives. Several homes and businesses were destroyed.

Edmonton Paranormal investigated a year or two after the fires and found themselves coming to the aid of a paramedic who was under a lot of stress, says Rogers. The paramedic had hurt her back lifting a particularly heavy patient, and her personal life was in turmoil.

When Rogers and a fellow investigator and psychic arrived, they found the paramedic was experiencing a typical haunting, with strange footsteps heard in the home, and objects moving about on their own. What was strange to Rogers and her colleague was the lack of any real presence in the home.

"When we walked into the house, we actually felt nothing. Normally you'll pick up on something. Something feels off. You get a general feel for what is actually happening. But, on a mediumship level, there was nothing," she says.

Determined to help, Rogers and her partner set up cameras and went about investigating in the usual fashion, interviewing the paramedic and others involved in the case, touring the home, and conducting EVP sessions.

The investigation lasted throughout the weekend, with nothing in particular standing out to the investigators. Then, while sitting in a guest room with the client, Rogers heard footsteps come up the stairs. Big, heavy footsteps, like someone was wearing boots.

The other investigator was asleep in another part of the house, so at first Rogers thought it might be him, she says. Even though, in the back of her mind, she suspected otherwise. So she got up and walked downstairs to speak with him.

Rogers peered into the room where her partner was sleeping, and, sure enough, he was still asleep.

She ran back upstairs to rejoin the client. Almost as soon as she sat down, the footsteps came up the stairs again.

"This was a single dwelling, so there were no other homes attached. There was no reason for the noise," says Rogers.

A couple of seconds later, there was a loud crash. Rogers and the client investigated and found a vase that'd been resting on a shelf near the stairs had fallen to the ground.

"Of course, the client freaked out," says Rogers.

Another encounter Rogers had with whatever was inside the house occurred as she was trying to fall asleep. Rogers was staying in one of the guest bedrooms and was lying on the floor on a mattress. As she lay there, she felt the bottom of the air mattress sink to the floor, as if someone had sat down on it.

"At first, I thought it was the other investigator, so I said, 'What do you want?'" she says.

Rogers opened her eyes and looked. No one was there, she says. Nor had any other part of the air mattress lost any air.

One of the client's other claims was her dogs, which were left in cages when she went to work, would be trembling with fear whenever she came home, as if they were terrorized by a presence in the house. So the investigators put the dogs in their cages, trained a couple of video cameras on them, and let the cameras roll while everyone in the house left for a couple of hours.

When they returned, Rogers and company found the dogs exactly as the client described – they were huddled in the backs of their cages and trembling. She says the dogs were Chihuahuas and prone to trembling anyway, so the investigators were still skeptical.

Then they watched the tape.

The footage captured the sounds of everyone leaving the house. A few minutes later, footsteps could be heard walking up to the cages, prompting the dogs to bark at whoever, or whatever, was approaching.

"You can see them start to tremble, see them back up in their cages, and you hear this weird growling. The thing is the growling is not coming from the dogs. The growling is coming from outside the cage," says Rogers.

At that moment, Rogers was convinced something was going on in that house.

Whatever it was took things up a notch the next day, including cupboards and drawers opening on their own, she says. What confused Rogers was she and her colleague were still unable to psychically pick anything up inside the house.

"We had to go completely off the evidence," she says, which was mounting.

By this point, the client was a complete mess, says Rogers. To the point where she was jumping at every little movement or sound, believing it to be paranormal.

So Rogers called in other investigators to help. When they arrived, she directed everyone to investigate outside the home while she and the client remained inside. Her thinking was she and the client could have a quiet coffee and chat, and see what happens, while the rest of the team monitored things from outside, where they were out of sight.

Before long, Rogers and the client heard the footsteps on the stairs and banging on the walls. Then one of the outside investigators phoned Rogers on her cellphone, asking if she or the client had just looked out the window.

"No. We're sitting at the kitchen table," she told him.

"The blinds literally just opened," the investigator informed Rogers. "You need to get out of the house right now! There's something seriously wrong with this house!"

In the end, Rogers and the client left the home.

After some time to reflect, Rogers and the team became convinced the client had created a poltergeist. As discussed in a previous chapter, a poltergeist is a spirit that bangs on walls and opens cupboards, with the activity focused around a female, usually an adolescent going through puberty.

The paramedic wasn't a teenager, but her life was in turmoil, and she was experiencing physical pain as well as depression. Rogers believes there was enough negative energy there to bring about poltergeist activity. This too would explain her inability to pick up on a presence psychically.

"Usually, if I'm having a paranormal experience, I get the chills. I get cold. The hair stands up on the back of my neck," she says. "You know the signs of something happening."

The client's husband had been out of town for work. When he returned, Rogers approached him, showed him what evidence Edmonton Paranormal had compiled, and suggested sharing the experience with their local priest. Rogers also recommended the client seek help from a counsellor.

"Not because she was crazy, but because that anxiety was really building up and creating that activity," she says. "There was no doubt something was happening in this home."

Thankfully, the client did meet with a counsellor as well as the family's priest, says Rogers. The couple contacted Edmonton Paranormal a year later, and the activity had died down considerably. As Rogers had hoped, so had the client's anxiety and depression, which she suspects was the cause of the disturbance.

Given her psychic and scientific approach to investigating the paranormal, Rogers does have her theories about what is going on around her. She believes people do pass on to another place when they die, but that time passes differently on the other side. That's why a building might appear to be haunted for two hundred years, but to the spirits living there, it's only been a few minutes. This could explain why some of the ghosts she has encountered think they're still living in the past, when in actuality a hundred or more years have gone by.

She suspects spirits stay in places that mean something to them, and doesn't believe in cleansing a home or historical site in order to end activity. Rogers would rather find another means to bring a client peace, or leave such a decision up to them.

For Rogers, her abilities aren't any sort of burden at all. Instead, they are another means of understanding the world around her, she says. And she's determined to keep bringing that understanding to others who experience unexplained activity in their homes for as long as she can.

13 JOHN MOORE

Growing up in a family of undertakers, it seems logical John Moore's life would lead him on the path of researching what happens when we die.

He was no stranger to death, having spent a good part of his youth in and around the funeral home that made his family's business. And, given his close proximity to dead people, it would only be a matter of time until the young Moore had his first spectral encounter.

This took place when Moore was eight years old, and occurred after a wake. Moore's dad was cleaning up in the chapel, and he was waiting in the foyer. Downstairs was a casket showcase room with another room off to the side where bodies were kept if there was more than one in the funeral home. From where Moore was sitting, he could see down the stairs to the showcase room.

Something caught Moore's eye at the bottom of the stairs, so he turned and looked. Standing there was an old man, who smiled and waved at him.

Moore waved back and said hello. The man turned and walked out of view.

Drawn by his son's greeting, Moore's dad stepped out of the chapel and asked whom he was speaking to. Moore told his dad there was a man downstairs, which his dad thought was odd, as everyone from the wake should have left. So his dad went to investigate, in case one of the guests had gotten lost on their way out.

"It turns out, there was no one there," says Moore.

Who Moore saw remained a mystery for a couple of years, until he and his grandmother were browsing through some family photo albums. Flipping through the pages, they came across a picture of the man Moore saw at the base of the stairs in the funeral home. He pointed the man out to his grandmother, who had some startling information to share.

"Turns out that's my great-grandfather, who was the one who built and opened the funeral home," he says. "He passed away three months before I was born."

Moore's great-grandfather was a believer in the paranormal, and given the line of work they were in, the family experienced otherworldly strangeness all their lives. No one was surprised when young Moore said he saw a ghost, nor that it was his great-grandfather.

In fact, his great-grandfather always told his family the dead wouldn't bother them because they were the undertakers who give them their final dignity, he says.

"We give them the chance for closure and to say goodbye. That's why he said the dead don't bother us," says Moore.

Although his interest was piqued, Moore was still eight years old, and other interests quickly attracted his attention. It wasn't until he was fifteen and encountered a spectre that had been seen a total of two thousand times that the paranormal became his lifelong obsession.

His family had moved into another house in Perth-Andover, New Brunswick, Canada, a smaller town of about fifteen hundred residents. The home was previously owned by a Mr. Farmer, who had long since passed away. In life, Farmer was often seen by passersby standing in the big bay window that looked out over the road in front of his house, and the river that ran beside it.

In death, Farmer was still seen standing in that same window by passing motorists, cyclists, and those out for a stroll, which accounts for the sheer volume of witnesses, says Moore.

"He would always have his hand up on that window, and there was a handprint on that window," he says.

No matter what anyone did to remove the hand-print, it would always reappear. Moore says his girlfriend at the time, who is now his wife, even tried cleaning the hand-print away. Moore told her to wait and watch, as the print would eventually return.

She watched for ten minutes before turning to Moore and asking him what she was supposed to see, he says. When she turned back to the window, the hand-print had returned.

"It doesn't come back right away, but it's like it's burned in. It'll wait until no one is looking, and then it'll reappear," he says.

Moore saw Mr. Farmer with his own eyes one night when he fell asleep on the living room sofa while watching the hockey game. He woke up and turned to the bay window with a start. Farmer was standing there!

Farmer turned and looked at Moore, then walked to the staircase, went upstairs, and disappeared, he says.

He's not the only one to encounter Farmer's ghost first hand. A previous resident, who was half Indigenous, saw him too. Moore says Farmer was alive in the late 1800s and early 1900s and wouldn't have taken kindly to the concept of an interracial marriage. He believes the resident, whose father was native and mother Caucasian, didn't approve of that family living in his house.

The previous resident told Moore that Farmer's spirit would come into his bedroom at night and hit his legs repeatedly. The blows were so hard, the boy had welts, says Moore.

"He believes he [Farmer] was being mean to him because he was interracial," he says. "That was one story about that place that was actually shocking."

By now, Moore was old enough to take a serious interest in the paranormal. He began going to the library and taking out books on the subject, especially volumes by Hans Holzer and Ed and Lorraine Warren.

"I would read anything I could get my hands on," says Moore. "That was most of the stuff I was able to find in the mid nineties."

He also started conducting his own investigations, just little ones here and there, as he describes them. One such outing took place behind the town's courthouse at the Hanging Tree, a large, ominous tree where hangings took place in the early 1800s. Moore spent many nights sitting under the Hanging Tree with a tape recorder, hoping to capture a ghostly voice on audio.

"Never did catch anything there, unfortunately," he says.

As time passed, Moore started investigating local museums with a haunted reputation, plus homes where people reported hearing strange noises and seeing lurking shadows. He says Perth-Andover was, and remains, rich with such stories because it was where the first settlers lived in Canada.

As he grew up, his investigations took him to St. Andrews by-the-Sea, a small town and historical site in New Brunswick. There, he recorded a warm footprint with his thermal camera on the otherwise cold floors of a jailhouse. His colleague on the investigation screamed moments later, saying she'd seen a full-body apparition. Moore says she was so frightened by the experience they had to leave.

St. Andrews by-the-Sea is also home to the Algonquin Hotel, which is rumoured to be one of the most haunted hotels in Canada. The spirits said to walk the property – which has a mock-Tudor style similar to the Overlook Hotel in Stephen King's *The Shining* – include the Night Watchman, who's jingling keys announce his presence, a bellman who greets guests in the hallways, and a weeping bride who spooks anyone staying in room 473.

One of Moore's favourite St. Andrews locales is Hospital Island, which he and his team, Ottawa Paranormal Research and Investigations, are scheduled to investigate once COVID-19 restrictions ease.

Located about a mile from shore, the island is where turn-of-the-century immigrants infected with scurvy were basically left to die. Nothing grows there, and the only structure is a half-built house. The townsfolk refuse to set foot on the island, and fishermen avoid it at all costs, says Moore.

"Anyone who's gone there has had serious health issues or died," he says.

One local did set foot on Hospital Island with his two dogs. As the story goes, one of the dogs vanished almost before his eyes and couldn't be found. Moore says the man returned to shore with his remaining dog and, six months later, killed himself.

The partially built home was an attempt by the island's owners to defy the stories and settle there. His wife, an expert skier, was skiing with her kids on a family-friendly trail and died when she somehow collided with a tree.

Two months later, the husband died of a heart attack. Moore says the man had no pre-existing health conditions.

"I've got clearance from their daughter, who owns it, and I've found a vessel willing to take us there, drop us off, and then come pick us up in the morning," says Moore. "We are actually going!"

Despite the many places Moore has been to, his favourite investigation took place at his old home in Perth-Andover long after the family had moved out. The team was using a Spirit Box, which Moore usually discounts because the device can create audio pareidolia. Given the small-town setting and late hour, he was inclined to use it because no radio stations in the area broadcast after midnight, which he believed reduced the odds of anything interfering with the Spirit Box.

Moore asked if anyone was in the room beside him, and a woman's voice replied, "Yes." He also asked if any past owners were present, and a voice said, "Jean-Guy."

Jean-Guy worked at a local restaurant and died in the house. People thought he'd committed suicide, but Moore also heard Jean-Guy had fallen in with a bad crowd and had been murdered by bikers, he says. Jean-Guy's body had been found hanging from the rafters in the room Moore and his team conducted the EVP session in.

"They were in town for three days looking for him, and on the day they left, they found his body," says Moore. "There's a large number of people who believe he was murdered in that house."

Moore had a digital video camera set up in one of the bedrooms, which used to belong to his sister. The footage shows Moore and company conducting their investigation. But Moore's thermal camera picked up what looks like part of a dress sweeping into frame and walking through the room.

No such thing showed up on the digital-camera footage, he says.

"Twenty-five years of doing this, and I've hardly caught any video evidence. That was definitely one of the best bits of video evidence I've ever got," says Moore.

Like many serious investigators, Moore prefers to stick with tried-and-true equipment like digital recorders and cameras. He shies away from any kind of electromagnetic field detector because there's too many variables involved that might not be paranormal.

"We do check out EMF spikes and things like that, but most of the time we're able to determine where they're coming from. We use them more for environmental data as opposed to ghost detection," he says.

The newest piece of equipment he's acquired is a laser audio system. This is based on spy technology from the 1960s and sends out a laser beam that covers a surface, picks up sound vibrations, and transmits them back to a receiver so any audio can be heard. Moore is excited to try it, as long as he's careful with where he aims the beam, keeping in mind it will pick up any sound vibration.

Moore has found himself in the enviable – to some at least – position of his team being featured on their own television show. *Into the Haunting* filmed a couple of episodes before the pandemic hit, and there are a couple of networks circling the project.

"The series follows my team and me around. We investigate; we show people how we investigate," he says.

His goal is to portray investigations as accurately as possible without resorting to the usual reality show formula of false scares, says Moore. At the same time, he wants to have fun with the formula too.

"There are a couple of times when you'll hear us go 'What was that? Oh, nothing'. Then someone will go 'I didn't hear anything either'," he says, and laughs. "We play around with it like that, and have some fun with it."

So far *Into the Haunting* has focused on lesser known historical locations in hope of drawing more visitors to these spots. Moore says it's about preserving history as well as entertaining fans of ghosts and high strangeness.

Speaking of which, an *Into the Haunting* investigation prompted a couple of employees at a small tavern to quit because of a spooky encounter. Moore says the ghost of a deceased pianist was believed to haunt the tavern, so he and his team brought a keyboard along in hope of making contact.

During an EVP session, with the keyboard close by, one of the investigators asked if the pianist could play something for them as a way of giving a sign of her presence. All of a sudden, the keyboard started going off. Everyone began asking each other if they were responsible, because no one could believe the keyboard was playing by itself, he says.

"No one was within five feet of it," says Moore. "The guy who owns the keyboard said it's never done that before, and it's never done it since."

No matter if he's trying to help frightened home-owners or entertain on television, Moore says his job isn't to debunk anything, because debunking means proving something isn't there. If someone is having an experience, it means something is happening, be it paranormal or otherwise. His job is to find out what.

"It is nice when we can get into a place where there is something supernatural so we can document it, interact with it, and get some semblance of what happens when our corporeal form dies and we move on to something ethereal," he says.

In a way, Moore is carrying on the family tradition of caring for those who died, having traded a funeral home for a digital recorder and camera. And it's a tradition he plans to continue with until he gets that final answer to what happens to us when we die.

14   KRISTEN PERKINS

Up until her son was four weeks old, Kristen Perkins had pretty much reasoned every potential paranormal experience away.

Then came the afternoon when she put her son down in the middle of her and her husband's bed in order to get his crib ready for a nap, and the television, which was on, turned itself off.

That gave her pause, but she told herself things like this do happen. So she carried on about the business of getting her son ready for bed.

And the television turned itself back on.

"Well, that's weird," she said to herself.

Shaking her head, she went to leave the room so she could get some bedding... and the television turned off again!

Undeterred, she put her son down for his nap and went about her day. She mentioned what had happened to her husband when he got home from work at the nearby military base, saying she believed there was an electrical problem in the house.

He asked why she thought that, and as Perkins started to answer, she was pinched on the back of the leg by an unseen hand. This prompted her to scream and run across the room. Her husband, still dressed in his army fatigues, could only watch, dumbfounded.

"Calm down. Everything's fine. It might have just been static or something," he told her after she explained why she'd run screaming across the room. "Let's sit down and talk this through."

Perkins sat down on the couch in the living room, her husband in a chair across from her. Just as she's about to explain her day a pen, which rested on the coffee table between them, rolled from one end of the table to the other without provocation and then all the way back.

"Now he's freaking out," Perkins says years later. "And, in his full military gear, climbing over me to get away."

Perkins says she and her husband spent the rest of the day explaining what had happened away, and went to bed, hoping to sleep the whole thing off. She admits they both felt pretty silly about it in the morning.

She was blow drying her hair in the bathroom, and he was changing their son in the baby's room, while they talked through the previous day's events. She turned to speak to her husband, and saw the dresser in the baby's room lift off the floor, fly across the room, and slam into the wall, spilling all the drawers and clothes onto the floor.

Her husband ran from the house screaming, she says.

"That was pretty profound," says Perkins. "It was a big, heavy bureau, and it picked itself up and threw itself across the room."

This all took place in 1994 in West Texas. Perkins says no one wanted to hear about what happened, or talk about it. The paranormal was still a taboo subject, and those you did try to talk about it to didn't want to talk to you again.

"They thought I was into bad things. That I was a Satanist or I was crazy. There was no way that would happen," she says.

"But it happened."

This event stuck with Perkins. For her, it was a profound development in her life and world view. And when something profound happens, people do two things. Her husband chose to ignore it and never spoke about it again. Perkins, on the other hand, became fascinated with the paranormal.

"For me, I had to know more. It's kinda what drove me from then on to find out what happened. To find some answers," says Perkins.

She didn't jump into the world of investigations until 2003, when she and her family had relocated to Massachusetts. She was in the living room one night watching television, and a show came on about ghost hunting. For Perkins, it was her "Aha" moment.

"I thought 'What? People do this?' And I was hooked because finally there was a way to start finding some answers," she says.

Perkins was able to track down a group of local ghost hunters and join the team. But she was part of a military family, and her husband was eventually transferred to Oklahoma. She joined a paranormal investigation group there, but found the members put a heavy focus on psychic impressions, which isn't how she approaches investigations.

It's not that Perkins doesn't believe in psychic abilities. She says there are genuine people out there who have the ability to tap into the world around us and communicate with the dead. But there are also people out there who claim to be psychic but aren't. These people prey on the misfortunes of others and take advantage of those who are grieving and want to speak to a dead loved one, and make money off them.

Those who are legitimate have a real gift, says Perkins. She recalls an encounter with the real deal many years ago. Perkins was ready to prove she was a hoax, and the woman took her up on the challenge. As Perkins describes it, she was schooled by this woman, who revealed personal information about Perkins that would have been impossible for her to know – like everything that had gone on in Perkins's West Texas home that night in 1994!

The psychic told her a Hispanic man with the initials RQ was responsible for the night's activity, Perkins says. This jogged a memory for her: she worked at the local hospital at the time of the haunting, and one of her patients, who had the initials RQ, passed away just before that profound night.

When Perkins asked why RQ would react so violently to her in her home, the psychic told her he wasn't trying to scare her, but get her attention, she says.

"That has really stuck with me, because I think a lot of things we're afraid of in this field – I don't get rattled that easily anymore – that's just fear of what we don't understand, and I didn't understand what was happening back then, and it terrified me. But he was just trying to get my attention," says Perkins.

So Perkins started her own group, Insight Paranormal, in 2006 and has been investigating ever since.

Insight Paranormal has investigated many cases over the years and compiled some interesting experiences and evidence. But, as is the case, one stands out for Perkins, and it's one she doesn't share very often, as she's afraid people will think she's crazy.

The team was called to a house in Shawnee, Oklahoma, where the family was experiencing all types of frightening activity. Perkins says the son was having suicidal thoughts and not only wanted to harm himself, but the family dog as well. Everyone was fighting depression and arguing, and reported a heavy feeling throughout the home.

So Perkins and a team drove out to Shawnee for an overnight investigation. It didn't take long for the investigators to have their own experiences.

"We all heard this almost corny-sounding evil laugh, like from a movie," she says.

At one point, Perkins began to feel physically sick, so a team member took a picture of her. When she looked at the photograph a while later, it appeared a blue mist had enveloped her midsection.

Halfway through the night, Perkins was overcome by a feeling of panic and decided she needed some air. So she went outside, took a deep breath, and turned around to face the house.

And it looked completely different than the home she'd just stepped out of.

"The paint color was different. The light fixtures appeared different. Everything about it was different," says Perkins. "It went from a white house to a yellow house."

She literally gave her head a shake, and the house returned to the way it had been moments before.

As if that wasn't startling enough, a voice seemed to whisper in her right ear, "This is my house!"

This rattled Perkins. So much so she took off all her equipment and put it on the ground. Then she took out her cellphone, walked away from the house, and phoned Jason Hawes to get some advice.

Perkins is a member of TAPS, The Atlantic Paranormal Society founded by Jason Hawes and Grant Wilson of *Ghost Hunters* fame, and is the family manager for the investigative teams that are a part of it. This includes Insight Paranormal.

Hawes put her in touch with Adam Berry, who'd had some experience with encounters where people's perceptions are manipulated. Perkins says that was the only time such a thing happened to her.

"It's alarming to think that something can change the way you see something," Perkins says. "It was the strangest experience I've had."

Perkins asked Berry what she could do to protect herself and her team throughout the rest of the investigation. Berry surprised her by questioning why she would want to go back inside. When she responded there was clearly something there, he came back with a simple retort.

"Do you need more evidence of that, or do you now believe that something's there? Why would you go back?" he asked.

Although that was by far the most profound experience Perkins has had as an investigator, her career – and association with TAPS – has taken her to some well-known haunted locations, like the notorious Waverly Hills Sanatorium in Jefferson County, Kentucky, which is home to numerous spirits.

As is the case with many high-profile locations with a reputation for being haunted, most like Waverly Hills don't deliver the goods on a regular basis, says Perkins. It's the residential and commercial investigations like the one detailed above that stick with her.

One TAPS visit brought her to Whispers Estate, which is rumoured to be the most haunted place in Indiana and has been featured on various paranormal television shows. Spirits rumored to reside there include ten-year-old Rachel Gibbons, whose footsteps are said to still pitter-patter through the halls and up the stairs. Perkins was facilitating this TAPS event, which allowed locals to join in the investigation.

She walked into one of the bedrooms where team members and the public were taking part in an EVP session, and was about to tell everyone it was time to move on to the next room. A woman among the group asked if they could wait a moment, as the mood of the room had suddenly become heavy, says Perkins.

At that moment, a beach ball that had been resting on the bed launched across the room and bounced off the wall, much to everyone's shock, she says.

"They all got their money's worth that night," says Perkins.

When on these investigations, Insight Paranormal gathers the usual EVPs and photographic evidence if any presents itself. Perkins and company also developed a device called the Transducer, which plugs a copper coil into a microphone to record EMF.

Although the Transducer doesn't pick up voices – you can scream beside the microphone and no sound will register – the device once picked up a voice speaking in Spanish at a remote location, Perkins says.

"What I heard was Anita escritoire, and I was standing beside a desk. Maybe it was Anita's desk?"

Despite this high-tech tool, Perkins prefers a digital recorder and a pad of paper to write down her findings. As many investigators find, it's the simple gadgets that bring the best results. But, if needed, Insight Paranormal has pretty much every piece of paranormal equipment at its disposal.

"We have way too much gear," she says.

Even with all she's seen and experienced, Perkins isn't a hard believer in ghosts. But she says she's open to the possibility they are real. So what does she think is going on at all these locations she's visited over the years?

"I'm just not sure," she says, adding any evidence she or others find proves nothing. It's all just in support of a belief.

"I'm pulled between the metaphysical side and the science side of things."

One concept she's willing to accept is the multiverse, which we've touched on elsewhere in this book. Perkins believes the concept could explain everything from ghosts to UFOs and cryptids.

But, until an answer is conclusively found, Perkins and Insight Paranormal will continue to look for answers no matter where the road takes them.

15 LOUISE SETCHELL

For investigator Louise Setchell, it was a natural curiosity, and a terrifying childhood experience, that launched her career in the paranormal.

"I've always had this natural affinity to be drawn toward the paranormal, because it's the natural curiosity that I have of what's going on, what happens when we die," says Setchell. "We can explain so much in the world, but we cannot explain this. We still can't explain what happens after we die."

This affinity stems all the way back to Setchell's childhood, when she was growing up in Leamington, England. She recalls reading Stephen King's *It* and other horror novels when she was ten years old, and playing with Ouija boards throughout her teenage years.

Many paranormal investigators interviewed in this book have expressed a similar interest in horror movies and novels, especially at a young age when such entertainment was deemed taboo. Setchell says being drawn to "things that are not right" came natural to her and sparked a curiosity she still has today.

Many of her friends were also driven to play with Ouija boards, and the group often passed after-school and weekend hours attempting to communicate with spirits. This extracurricular activity led to a couple of unexplainable encounters that stuck with Setchell the rest of her life.

The most frightening occurred in her childhood home, which was constructed back in the 1800s. The home was built with heavy wooden doors and solid oak panelling. It creaked a lot, she says. And, being a rural home, it had a huge garden that backed onto a farmer's field.

On this particular night, Setchell sat in her bedroom, pondering the suicide of someone close to her.

"It wasn't sitting well with me, and I was trying to process it," she says. "So one night, I decided I was going to use a Ouija board, and I'm going to talk to that person."

She took out a piece of paper and drew a Ouija board.

Using a glass as a planchette, Setchell began asking the usual questions: is anyone there? What is your name?

Suddenly, the glass started going crazy, darting back and forth across the homemade Ouija board!

"I can't control it. It was like there was this weird force controlling it," says Setchell. "Honestly, there was nobody else in the room. It was just me. And I couldn't understand what was going on."

Barely able to control the planchette, she let go. The glass flew across the carpeted room and rolled underneath Setchell's bed.

Not knowing what to make of the experience, Setchell decided to put a movie on and go to bed. However, given she was shaken by the night's events, she was unable to fall asleep despite feeling utterly exhausted.

Setchell slept on a metal-framed bunk bed, which had a double bed on the bottom and a single bed on top. She lay on the bottom, tossing and turning. Then she heard scratching from beneath the mattress, like fingernails clawing at the metal slats that held the mattress.

At first, she shrugged the sound off as rats. Her family did live in an old house in the country, after all, she says. But she refused to peer under the bed, because fear had gripped her.

"I'm lying there, and the scratching stops. Then I can start to feel like these hands pushing me up on the mattress. And they are right in the middle of my back, and it feels like one hand on one side, then the other, then the other side..." she says.

"And then I just get pushed up!"

The entire bed frame started shaking and rattling so hard it started banging on the wall. This went on for several minutes. The noise was so loud it woke her alcoholic stepmother from a drunken slumber, says Setchell. Then it stopped.

"The room just felt dark. It was as if all the electricity had been lost across the world, and it was pitch black in my room. It wasn't that dark when all of this started," Setchell says of the calm afterward.

It was then that the step-mother stormed into the room in a daze, and demanded to know what the hell her step-daughter was up to.

Instead of answering, Setchell grabbed her duvet and ran downstairs and slept on the sofa. She says she refused to sleep in that room again. Her dad and step-mother set up another bedroom for her in the house.

Setchell's step-brother ended up moving into the room, and found the planchette glass smashed under the bunk bed. Setchell says the glass wasn't smashed when it rolled under the bed.

To this day, she still can't explain what could have caused all that to happen. An old house creaks and groans, but no house settling can cause a bed to do that. And she says earthquakes just don't happen in England. Never mind the crazy darkness that inhabited the room once the shaking had settled down.

The experience never left Setchell's mind and drove her interest in spooky things toward what was to her the very real world of the paranormal. She began watching the popular British reality series *Most Haunted*, which sparked an investigative interest in her and had her wanting to investigate the paranormal.

This interest stuck with her when she moved to Canada in 2010. She currently lives in Vancouver, British Columbia, and has a career in mental health. About eight years ago her passion for the television programs spilled over into the real world, and Setchell and a friend began purchasing equipment with the intent of doing their own investigations. The two even began researching potential locations for them to investigate together.

"I bought them out of absolutely everything," Setchell says of the GhostStop website. "I got everything I possibly could."

Her first purchases included a Spirit Box, a couple of voice recorders, and a video camera.

At the time, Setchell worked in geriatric psychology at Riverview, a mental health facility in Coquitlam, British Columbia, that shuttered its doors in 2012. Setchell had many strange experiences while working the night shift, and returned with her friend and brand-new ghost-hunting equipment in tow once it closed.

"I got some of the most incredible EVPs I've ever got in my time," she says of that first outing. "And this is what really sparked my interest. And I wanted to find other people who wanted to do it with me."

So Setchell began looking for people to investigate with, and places they could safely go and explore. Her quest eventually led her to Vancouver Paranormal Society and president Peter Renn. She remained with Vancouver Paranormal until 2020, when she helped co-found the

Canadian Paranormal Foundation with Renn and Jason Hewlett.

As the years passed, Setchell racked up a long list of investigations at various locations through the Lower Mainland and Interior of British Columbia, many of which provided memorable personal experiences and evidence.

But it's one encounter she had while working at Riverview before she became a serious investigator that sticks with her. Setchell worked a lot of night shifts, and that was when the large facility seemed most active.

One night, she headed up to the third floor to get some equipment. The floor was off-limits to patients, and all the doors were locked. Setchell says security staff were the only ones with keys to open any of the doors.

Setchell went to the third floor and peeked through a glass window to see if she could find what she needed – a large stretcher tub she could use to bathe one of her patients. She saw one poking out of a third-floor bedroom into the hallway, and headed back downstairs to phone security and get the door open.

Half an hour later security arrived, and the guard and Setchell climbed the stairs to the third floor. She wasn't allowed on the floor, but wanted to confirm the stretcher tub was still there, never mind there was no way anyone could've gone onto the floor and taken it without security being involved.

"I wanted to show them exactly where it was," she says.

Setchell looked through the glass in the door... and the stretcher tub was gone!

Security opened the door and went to investigate. Setchell asked if she could come too, but the guard declined, saying only security was allowed on this floor. She provided a description of the tub to the guard, who explored the floor. Setchell says the stretcher tub was nowhere to be found.

"I can't explain that," she says.

This was the most extreme experience Setchell had while working at Riverview, which developed a reputation as a haunted location in British Columbia's Lower Mainland. During her many night shifts, Setchell and other staff heard footsteps coming from the third floor and furniture moving about, no matter the floor was empty.

Similar noises were heard throughout the hospital during overnight shifts as well, she says. Staff reported seeing shadows move when no one was there, and equipment would seemingly move on its own and turn up in other parts of the hospital, much like the stretcher tub.

Elevator doors would open and close on their own, but only during the night. She says things like that never happened during the day.

Patients would do anything they could to avoid going into a certain room on the ward, but could never explain why the room gave them a sense of dread. Setchell says that same room was where many patients ended up passing away.

"The patients who were admitted into that room normally passed away within a week or two. They'd have nightmares and other experiences in the room before they died," she says.

There's another experience that stands out for Setchell, and this one took place after she started investigating with Vancouver Paranormal Society. The group was called to an alleged residential haunting in the city of Chilliwack, about an hour's drive east of Vancouver, and it was the team's second time at the home.

Throughout the night, Setchell felt a weird, tingling sensation on her back, like someone was constantly running a finger up and down her spine, she says. She thought it might be an allergic reaction to the dog hair that was present in the house, but notes she hadn't felt it during the team's first night at the home.

"I kept saying to everyone 'I feel something, and it's giving me shivers, and I can't explain it'," she says, adding others weren't experiencing the same thing.

Setchell had set up her camera, which was equipped with night vision, and had the lens aimed into the bathroom. She says this part of the house seemed quite active, and the team had gathered some compelling evidence there before.

While investigating, the team split off into smaller groups, each conducting EVP sessions in different parts of the house. When it was Setchell's turn to try to gather EVPs in the bathroom, she sat right smack dab in the middle of the active part of the room.

And not much of anything happened, Setchell says.

But, while reviewing evidence the next day, she heard something so shocking she ended up throwing her headphones across her apartment.

Throughout the footage, the viewer can see Setchell

sitting on the floor. You can see her lips move when she talks. At one point you can hear Setchell's voice say her full name – Louise Dawn Setchell – but her lips don't move!

"And none of you guys know my middle name. And why the hell would you be doing my accent and my voice," she wonders. "I just couldn't believe it."

Setchell even had a friend listen to the footage before she submitted it as evidence, and even he was dumbfounded by what he heard and saw. She says other Vancouver Paranormal investigators were also shocked by it.

That's not the only time a spirit has mimicked Setchell's voice. She and Peter Renn note a second time during a residential investigation that Setchell's voice turned up on audio, saying "turn the light off" when she was nowhere near the recorder's microphone.

"Those are freaky experiences, right? And I still carry on doing it!" she says, and laughs.

Setchell says she doesn't find any of these encounters frightening. The adrenalin of hearing a disembodied voice or seeing something unexplainable overrides any fear and drives her curiosity.

When it comes to the equipment she uses, Setchell, like most investigators, likes to keep it simple with her digital recorder and headphones. She counts EVPs among the most compelling evidence she's ever found, and that includes her solo investigations outside Riverview before joining Vancouver Paranormal Society.

What does Setchell think all this activity is about? She

doesn't know, which is why she's an investigator. Nor does she think anyone will ever know for sure.

"Is there something going on after you die? Yes. But why? I don't know," she says.

She doesn't believe everyone stays behind when they die; otherwise how many spirits would there be, walking around unseen beside us at all times? Setchell isn't sure that's possible.

But one thing is for sure, she intends to keep exploring old hospitals and residential homes in hope of finding out why some of us do stay behind, and some don't.

16 CODY CARLISLE

A dedicated paranormal investigator for the better part of a decade, Cody Carlisle has a hard time describing himself as a professional. In fact, as far as he's concerned, that term should never be used to describe anyone who takes the paranormal seriously.

And, he cautions, if someone comes up to you and says they're a professional paranormal investigator, it's probably best to run the other way.

"In the field, there really are no professionals. We're all students of the paranormal," says Carlisle.

Carlisle has belonged to various investigative groups over the years despite a stint in the United States military. He's been with Western Idaho Paranormal since 2012 and conducted investigations all around Idaho and Oregon with plans to expand elsewhere in the US.

Like so many students of the paranormal, Carlisle's education began as a child when he had a bedroom in the basement of his family's home, which was a farmhouse in rural Wyoming. He woke up suddenly in the middle of the night, he says. Looking down at him was an old woman, who reached out with one hand.

"The next thing I remember, I'm sitting up straight in bed, almost like I was awake, but I wasn't awake, and then I woke up, if that makes any sense at all?" Carlisle says.

"It was almost like in the movies, where you wake up into a dream, and then you wake up for real."

That morning at breakfast, Carlisle described his late-night visitor to his parents. His mother told him the woman he described resembled his grandmother, whom he hadn't seen since he was a baby. He says that stuck with him ever since and provided the inspiration for Carlisle to join other investigators on a variety of cases.

He's had two such cases he'd call profound, both since joining Western Idaho Paranormal. One doesn't stick out more than the other, but each is worth mentioning for a variety of reasons.

Western Idaho Paranormal had just completed a public-investigation event with the Thunder Mountain

Railroad, which travels cross country to Idaho City. Carlisle and two other investigators were riding the train home after explaining the investigative process to paying guests. The rest of the team were driving back in their personal vehicles, keeping relatively good pace with the train.

Carlisle says he was talking with another investigator when he heard someone try to get his attention. He distinctly heard someone say "Hey, Cody!"

He looked around, but no one seemed to want his attention. When he asked if anyone called his name, all those present said no, says Carlisle.

"The weird thing about it is it wasn't a random, unknown voice," he says. The voice was that of a former team member.

"It was very specifically that person's voice."

Thing is, there's no physical way it could have been that person trying to get Carlisle's attention at that time, as the teammate wasn't even on the train, but driving back in a vehicle!

"To this day, it remains unexplained. But it's a cool personal experience," says Carlisle.

At moments like this, it's up to an individual investigator's credibility when it comes to others believing what he or she says. Carlisle says his teammates took the experience at face value, which he appreciated at the time, as no one else heard the voice calling out to him.

The second standout moment occurred during a weekend-long investigation at the Sumpter Bed and Breakfast in Sumpter, Oregon. The home dates back to the early 1900s and used to be a hospital. Guests and employees alike have reported seeing two distinct apparitions on the premises. One is a miner who can be seen shaving in an upstairs bathroom, while the other is a shadowy spirit known as Jedidiah. His appearance is usually accompanied by disembodied footsteps and other strange noises.

Carlisle attended with other investigators, and the group had split up, with the majority of the team upstairs where the bedrooms and bath are located. Carlisle was on the main floor, which houses the kitchen and dining area, as well as the owner's accommodations.

The night had brought about some activity. Carlisle and two others were hesitant to leave, as they hoped to log some hard evidence, he says. The trio were seated in the common area when one of the group saw a shadowy figure peer out of the kitchen at them.

This prompted the three of them to get up and head for the kitchen. Carlisle says they got to the back of the kitchen, where a small booth is located. All at once, the three of them smelled cigar smoke mixed with an old machine-oil smell.

Carlisle paused and started sniffing around, going so far as to put his nose right on the table in hope of locating the source of the smell.

"I'm putting my nose on the table; I'm putting my nose on the wall," he says. "The smell would come, it would go, but it was really centred around that table."

While Carlisle sniffed away, one of the other investigators started seeing shadow-like figures dart about the kitchen, he says. Carlisle considers this a significant experience, given how everyone smelled the smoke and oil, and another team member witnessed shadow beings moving about.

When it comes to evidence gathered on an investigation, one standout case springs to Carlisle's mind. Western Idaho was investigating the Geiser Grand Hotel in Barker City, Oregon, where guests have seen ghosts lurking about all the way back to the early 1900s. Some of the most allegedly haunted parts of the hotel include the wine cellar, the tunnels beneath the building, and the third floor.

Carlisle says the spirit of a little girl is often seen in the hotel's basement, so he and a couple of other investigators set themselves up in a circle, with an EMF detector placed in the middle of them. It wasn't long before one of the investigators started seeing lights play across the walls and floor, and another spotted shadows moving where there shouldn't be any.

"All of a sudden, out of nowhere, the temperature just, like, suddenly dropped," says Carlisle.

All of the investigators had visited the Geiser Grand Hotel before and been in the basement. He says basements are naturally cold, but this was colder than they'd ever felt, and they all felt it.

The sudden temperature shifts, combined with what the other two investigators saw with the shadows and light, made for a compelling experience, says Carlisle. Although he's never seen an apparition per se, sounds and shadows make up the bulk of his paranormal encounters.

Given his personal experiences, Carlisle is inclined to count his senses – sight, sound, smell, touch – as his most reliable tools when it comes to interacting with the paranormal. This is in line with what early investigators relied on before all this fancy equipment came on the scene, along with the desire to come up with presentable evidence. Carlisle believes too few modern investigators truly trust them.

As for what's the cause of all this unexplainable activity? Carlisle really doesn't know. Like many, he's inclined to believe in a kind of parallel environment we go to when we die that's happening at the same time as ours. And sometimes, that reality and our current one "bleed" together, he says.

"To use an analogy of cars driving on the freeway. There's multiple cars at the same exact time, and a lot of the time when we're driving, we're so focused on ourselves that 'Oh, I didn't see that cop just pass me', if that makes any sense," he says. "It's there, we're just not in tune to it."

Carlisle is thankful for the times he's been able to tune into this parallel reality, and hopes to keep crossing paths with it as often as he can as he continues to search for answers to the unexplained.

17 KENNEY W. IRISH

What happens when a man mixes his passion for monsters with his equal love of punk rock music? Why, he becomes the Cryptopunkologist of course.

And Kenney W. Irish looks every bit the part of a Cryptopunkologist. Sporting a Gone Ghostin' shirt complete with Sasquatch in Ghostbusters' attire, his own hair styled in a Mohawk, Irish wears his personality and interests refreshingly on his sleeve. Or should I say armbands?

At first, one might take the Cryptopunkologist identity as some marketing ploy or look-at-me attention grab. But talk to the man for a minute or two, and it becomes clear – Kenney W. Irish is indeed the Cryptopunkologist.

Which isn't to say Cryptopunkologist isn't a clever marketing idea, especially for a rock musician and established author of children's books who also happens to spend his weekends looking for cryptids and writing about them as well.

"I could call myself a cryptozoologist, but there are so many people out there who deserve that title," says Irish. "But I try to be humble enough to say I'm not a Ken Gerhard. I'm not a Lyle Blackburn. I'm about half of what those guys are. So what am I gonna fill the other half with? What is my other passion?"

The term was coined by Gary Robusto, the head field researcher for the New York Bigfoot Society, of which Irish is a member and investigator. The two men had worked together for some time when Irish says Robusto just turned and looked at him one day and said: "Man, you're like the Cryptopunkologist."

And Irish, who spends his days in sales and marketing, knew he'd found his niche.

"That's marketing gold right there," he says. "I'm

taking my two major passions in life and putting them all together in one. I'm writing about cryptids. I love cryptids. But I love music."

Even more important is Irish didn't come up with Cryptopunkologist himself. As far as he's concerned, no self-respecting human being comes up with his own cool nickname. But the name has stuck, and all anyone has to do is Google Cryptopunkologist and they'll also find the work of Kenney W. Irish.

With so many people into the paranormal these days and shows like *Finding Bigfoot* popping up on streaming services everywhere, Irish knows it's important to stand out, especially if you're serious about your passion, which he is. His nickname helps him stand out a bit more than other researchers and investigators in a unique way.

"Everybody is a researcher now. Everybody is a crypto-zoologist," he says. "It went mainstream, and there's a lot of people out there doing a lot of good work."

Irish developed his dual passions while growing up in northern Vermont, near Lake Champlain, and thought the possibility, however remote, of large hulking monsters roaming the Earth to be one of the coolest concepts ever.

He was particularly a fan of Champ, the aquatic cryptid believed to live in Lake Champlain, he says. It helped that he was, and still is, a Godzilla fan and likened the lake monster to his own giant, nuclear-fuelled reptile.

"My imagination was just in front of me growing up. It was never behind me. When I was in school and was supposed to be paying attention, my mind was just wondering all over about this monster and that monster.

Which one was I going to be thinking about today? Which one was I going to be talking about today?" says Irish.

Irish developed a talent for writing, and while the other kids were diligently writing the book reports their teachers had assigned, he wrote about creatures lopping someone's head off. He says he wasn't so much the weird kid in class, but he was the guy who had the weird kid's back if needed.

Those early years became the driving force behind everything Irish does today. Even when he discovered it was no longer cool to talk about monsters, and he pushed the passion aside in pursuit of other interests, his love of Bigfoot, Champ and Godzilla remained, only more in the background.

In the foreground was a burgeoning interest in music and girls, he says. He remembers hearing a few licks from a Tommy James and the Shondells song and being completely hooked. This led him to harder and heavier bands like The Misfits, and Irish's love affair with punk rock was born.

It wasn't until his senior year in high school, while taking a writing course for credit so he could graduate, that his love of monsters came back into focus.

"My mind's just been off the grid from reality since then," says Irish.

Yet he was still several years away from taking his love of monsters into the realm of cryptozoology. Irish graduated and went to college. He settled down, started a career and took on all the responsibilities of adulthood.

Then a buddy of his suggested they start a band, which

Irish admits was a little ill timed, given most people get the whole rock-star dream out of the way before settling down, he says. Life became all about working during the week, then touring on weekends, essentially hitting the road Friday afternoons and returning home just in time to get back to the day job.

His band, Final Mile, proved quite successful and even produced a few albums before the grind of the music industry convinced Irish and company to disband. In its place, Irish found himself a father, and he spent a few years doing "the dad thing".

Eventually, the urge to write came back, and Irish didn't want to focus on writing music. So he started writing short stories and eventually penned a chapter book for kids called *Kevin and the Upside Down Halloween*, which was published in 2014 to strong sales.

This led to a second children's book, this one with a cryptid theme, called *Stanley Ryker and the Bigfoot Run Around*, which was published in early 2020. Irish then focused his attention on Sasquatch, the Mothman, Champ and other alleged monsters with *American Cryptids: In Pursuit of the Elusive Creatures*, which was published by Beyond the Fray Publishing.

As already alluded to, Irish doesn't just write about cryptids, he also investigates with the New York Bigfoot Society, a group of individuals who study, research and investigate a variety of alleged creatures in the region.

"We do investigate other cryptids, yet, when we go out into the field, we primarily investigate Sasquatch," he says.

Irish has been with New York Bigfoot Society for more

than two years, working alongside founder Gary Robusto, who's been a paranormal investigator for twenty-seven years, with cryptids holding his attention for the last twelve or so. Irish says he's learned a lot from Robusto, who is very knowledgeable when it comes to safely navigating the woods and presenting what passes for evidence in this pseudoscientific field.

Unlike many investigators, who focus on gathering any and all evidence they can in the present day, Irish prefers to look backwards at where the tales of these monsters began, most of which originated in Native American folklore.

"My background in monsters and research has mainly been everything from October 19, 1967, and back," he says, referencing the day prior to the release of the famous Patterson-Gimlin film, which is when most investigators and researchers begin their work.

"I credit most of what I've learned and what I've researched to the Native Americans."

Stories of Bigfoot and other monsters prevalent in pop culture today date back to the myths and legends of North America's first settlers, the Indigenous people. These tales were told orally and with pictographs and were often described as spirits or demons that dwelled in the forests and lakes. These stories are still taken seriously among today's Aboriginal cultures.

"The Native Americans always spoke on how, in some cases, they lived in unity with this other tribe of people, which they referred to as Sasquatch, wild man, or hairy man," says Irish. "Some tribes had different stories where children and women were taken in the night. There's definitely all kinds of different lore."

Whether spiritual beings or flesh-and-blood monsters, Irish has been on his share of expeditions into the woods in hope of an encounter or some kind of evidence of their existence. He says New York Bigfoot Society does some of the "Hollywood stuff" like tree knocks and calls, but they also do different things like setting up trail cameras and digital recorders all through the woods and leaving them running for hours.

His most memorable experience occurred early on a Thursday morning while in the deep woods. The group was hunkered down, discussing wood knocks. He says no two wood knocks created by people attempting to communicate with a Bigfoot ever sound the same. Yet those wood knocks allegedly caused by a Sasquatch always sound exactly alike.

"So we started testing different theories and started throwing rocks at trees, and every single time we got that same exact sound," says Irish. "One thing primates do is they clap rocks together, so we thought 'Hey, maybe we're onto something'."

Once the experiment ended, Robusto, who was by the fire at the group's base camp about five hundred yards away, radioed the others. He reported hearing something walking in the woods, Irish says. Everyone trained their flashlights and headlamps toward the noises, but couldn't see anything.

"The movement we were hearing, we're not saying it

was a Sasquatch, we're just saying we don't know what it was," he says.

So Robusto took a rock and threw it at a tree. WHACK!

About forty-five or fifty seconds later, everyone heard the exact sound come back. Irish says he could see everyone in the group via firelight or head lamp, and no one made the second sound. The two knocks were also captured by digital records set up in the trees.

"We were pretty psyched about that," he says, reiterating no one can prove the second knock was caused by a Bigfoot, they just can't explain it. "A lot of times, you don't hear anything back. To hear something back was exciting."

He says the group looked at a number of possible, logical explanations, including wind. Some times, when trees sway in the wind, they make a cracking sound that could be mistaken for a wood knock or a rock against a tree.

During another expedition into the woods, Irish and company decided to replicate how Native Americans attempted to communicate with Sasquatch. He says they brought a laptop and speakers and blasted Native American drumming into the dark.

"Not knowing, obviously, what we were going to get back from that, hoping we'd get some kind of response," says Irish.

They played the drumming for about thirty minutes, then switched it off and sat in silence, listening. In the distance, the group heard what sounded like something walking, he says. Two of the investigators swore whatever it was sounded like it was walking on two legs. All those years of playing live music made it hard for Irish to tell.

"To me, it just sounded like something moving," Irish says.

Then whatever it was stopped, and things went quiet. By then it was late, so the group packed up and walked back to their vehicles. Before getting into his, Irish paused and looked back to where they had been playing the music, and the area was bathed in a white light.

"It was right where we came from. There were no campers there. We thought maybe it was somebody walking through the woods with a flashlight, but it just stayed there. If someone was walking through the woods with a flashlight, they're going to be moving it," he says.

The spot was also a place the group frequently visited, so they knew there was no swamp gas or other possible cause, says Irish. Everyone stopped and watched. The white light would flicker, become less bright, then spark to life again. Eventually it faded to black.

To this day, no one in New York Bigfoot Society can explain what they saw, and they've since dubbed the phenomenon the Adirondack Lights after the region they conducted their research in. Irish says the group has encountered the lights since.

The Adirondacks are in Northern New York and comprise some six million acres of mountain peaks, sparkling lakes and wild space. A large number of Bigfoot and wild man sightings have been reported in the region and date back hundreds of years.

Irish wonders if the drumming in some way created

the lights, which for him means the event falls into the paranormal, something he admits he typically "runs screaming from". Some researchers believe Bigfoot is a paranormal phenomenon in and of itself and has a supernatural origin.

Robusto returned to that same spot, and all the batteries rapidly – and mysteriously – died on all his equipment. And one of his trail cameras started taking pictures for no reason and wouldn't stop... even when Robusto took the batteries out of it, says Irish. This continued for an additional twenty seconds after the batteries were removed.

"You can remove batteries, and it can still have a charge in there. It can still take another picture. Two pictures. But this went on for twenty seconds," says Irish.

He says Robusto's car battery was also completely drained, which shouldn't have been the case after driving a couple of hours to reach this location. There was so little charge left that, even when he was able to flag a passerby down, they were unable to jump-start it. In the end, the vehicle was towed back to the city.

There's a belief among many paranormal investigators that spirits can manipulate electronics to communicate or to give themselves the power to manifest. Pulling energy from batteries has been a common occurrence during an investigation, which is why investigators bring a good supply of batteries with them.

"Even though we go out and are looking more at things that are cryptids and Sasquatch like, there's still that paranormal, or should I say, ghost and spirit, atmosphere going on in the woods as well," Irish says.

On the equipment side of things, New York Bigfoot Society likes to keep it simple, says Irish. The team primarily uses trail cameras and digital recorders to conduct their research. They have Flare cameras as well, but all those do is point out deer or other wildlife in the distance.

So where does the Cryptopunkologist go from here? Irish says there will be more books and more expeditions into the deep woods. His love affair with the written word, monsters, and music has a lot of life left.

"That nickname speaks to, like, who I am. It describes me to a T. Anybody who knows me knows cryptids and music. That's my thing," he says. "Other than that, everything else is on the side."

18 ANGELA ARTUSO

Growing up, Angela Artuso had weird and unexplained things happen around her.

Then she became a teenager and started seeing dead people.

"And I'd physically see them," she says. "Whatever family relative would die, I would usually get a visitation within the first three days."

The experience is almost like a surreal, waking dream.

Artuso describes the night her father-in-law died. The family had met all day, planning the funeral and beginning to sort out the estate. She and her husband had gone to bed. Her sons were asleep in the room across the hall.

Artuso woke up in the middle of the night with a start, as if something jolted her awake. She rolled over and saw her father-in-law hovering beside the bed, visible from the thighs up, she says. He wore a suit and looked ten years younger and happy.

"He was encapsulated in some kind of glowing, holy light. And there was a tremendous noise in the room that was so loud. It was deafening. I could hardly hear. It was like a train roaring through our house," says Artuso.

The curtains were blowing about, and it was like the room was filled with a white static, like a television tuned to a dead channel. Artuso says she couldn't wake her husband up, no matter how hard she pushed and nudged him. Nor could she speak.

She doesn't remember falling back asleep. The next thing she knew it was morning, and she was awake, she says. Like she'd had one hell of a dream.

Artuso went downstairs to fix herself some coffee and waited. Her husband woke up first, and she told him what had happened. To her surprise, her husband told her he'd dreamed his father had come to visit him in their room and told him all the things he still had to take care of in life.

"Did you hear anything? Did you hear that noise?" she asked her husband.

"I heard nothing," he replied.

Then Artuso noticed her oldest son hadn't joined

them, and he was usually up by this time. So she went upstairs to check on him. The boy was in his bed, crying hysterically. She says he didn't even want to get out of his bed.

"I asked him what was wrong. Why are you crying?" she asked.

What her son said startled Artuso. He described waking up and seeing a bright, static-like light coming from his parents' room. There was a thunderous noise, and the curtains were blowing about. The boy couldn't get up, even though he wanted to run in and help, she says.

"So he saw it," Artuso says. "Whatever it was, he saw it. That was confirmation that whatever took place, took place. He saw it."

Artuso never understood how she was able to have these experiences, so she started reading books on the paranormal, including the work of Ed and Lorraine Warren. She wanted a better understanding of these supernatural phenomenon, she says.

She joined her first investigative group in 2006/2007 and essentially learned through her investigations and working alongside other teams with more experience. Her team was also able to connect with the TAPS family of investigators, which proved beneficial.

"We expanded and grew. We grew our thought process and grew our investigation techniques and looked for answers," says Artuso. "We investigate as much as we can, and come to conclusions as much as we can using numerous methods."

Artuso, along with her husband and now grown sons,

operate the Gotham Paranormal Research Society in New York, making it a family affair. She says the visit from her father-in-law impacted her family greatly.

She counts visitations from recently deceased relatives among her first paranormal experiences, including an encounter with her late grandfather during her teens. An encounter eerily similar to the one described at the beginning of this chapter. Artuso would also hear disembodied voices in places where no one was around. She says this is likely clairvoyance, which is the ability to gain information about an object, person, location or personal event through extrasensory perception and psychometry.

The more she explored these abilities and ventured into haunted locations, the more she came to understand her gift and how it could help others, she says.

Her personal encounters with the dead aside, Artuso counts an investigation at Burlington County Prison Museum in New Jersey among her most profound paranormal experiences, because it was the first time she encountered an apparition of someone outside her family.

The property is located next to Burlington County Jail in the Mount Holly Township of Burlington County, and reports of spirits roaming the prison date back to 1833. This was after the execution of Joel Clough, a murderer who was buried on the prison grounds. Guards and prisoners alike began hearing moaning and the rattling of chains coming from the basement dungeon. During renovations in the 1990s, workers would hear strange sounds and saw apparitions move about the building. Tools would go missing and turn up elsewhere. A steady stream of paranormal investigators has visited the prison museum since, Gotham Paranormal among them.

Artuso and her team were walking one of the hallways when they saw a blue silhouette of a woman in a gown come down a flight of stairs towards them... and just disappear before her eyes, she says.

"I was stunned," she says.

"In my previous years, I'd seen people who had passed on and had died, and I saw them in their human form. This was the first time I saw something silhouetted in a blue, glowing light coming towards me in a place you'd never expect to see a woman – in a prison, walking down steps. It was bizarre."

It took quite a while for Artuso to process the apparition, and the encounter remains burned into her mind to this day.

"I still can't figure out what caused it. There weren't any lights on in the prison," she says, adding the encounter took place at one in the morning. "All we had were our infrared lights and our equipment. That's it. Nothing that could cause a silhouette."

Also memorable is one of Artuso's first investigations, which took place at Katie's of Smithtown in Long Island. The bar has a long and storied haunted history and was featured on A&E's reality series *Paranormal State*. Glasses flying off the bar, strange footsteps, and people getting sudden chills are attributed to a variety of spirits, including Charlie Klein. Klein owned a hotel where the bar now stands and committed suicide at the location in the 1920s.

Other spirits have been seen on the property, including

a black mass in the basement said to create feelings of negativity. Voices of women and children are heard by the current owner and his staff.

Artuso says the hotel burned down on December 5, 1909, and it's unknown if anyone was trapped inside and died. But one can definitely "feel", for lack of a better word, when you cross over from the new construction to where the original hotel once stood.

"You can't explain it. We don't know what causes it. But everybody who goes to that side of the room, when they cross that dividing line where the old foundation ends to the new tile and the new foundation, you actually feel a heavy, heavy presence down there," she says.

Gotham Paranormal has witnessed glasses flying off the rack, says Artuso. And that happened in front of a crowd of people attending a preview of one of the many ghost-hunting shows the bar has been featured on.

"We were all sitting at the bar, and that happened," she says. "It was like 'Here we go again'!"

While setting up for the team's first investigation at Katie's, the investigators noticed some equipment had gone missing – in particular some EMF detectors. Artuso says the devices had been left on a table but vanished. When asked, none of the team members could account for them.

A quick search of the bar turned up two of them, but a third piece of equipment was still missing. Needing to get started, the team commenced the investigation. Then, about three-quarters of the way through the night, Artuso's husband's jacket suddenly slumped off the back of the chair it was resting on and fell to the floor.

Inside the jacket pocket was the last missing piece of equipment, says Artuso. And it was turned on!

"It was the most bizarre thing ever," Artuso says.

That same night, while investigating and filming downstairs, Artuso thought she saw something in a large mirror. Now, this mirror is at the bottom of a flight of stairs where the bar's owner claimed he had a strange encounter. The owner had been working on the security door at the top of the stairs and fell. As his body hit the floor at the bottom of the stairs, he claims something cradled his head in order to prevent it from smashing into the concrete floor.

Gotham Paranormal had a camera facing the stairs, and Artuso was standing by it. She says something caught her eye, but was there and gone in an instant. Once the investigation was over, she checked the camera roll and it had recorded what looked like a scarf-wearing boy standing where Artuso thought she saw something earlier that night.

Who the boy was, Artuso isn't sure. None of her research suggests a boy died in the hotel fire or anywhere near where the bar now stands, she says.

Skeptics believe trains rolling through a nearby station are responsible for the activity at Katie's, especially the flying wine glasses and items falling off tables and shelves. Gotham Paranormal decided to test that theory. They set up motion sensors along the bar and on several tables and waited for trains to roll through.

None of the alarms went off, nor did any glasses go flying across the room. She says investigators even stood coins on their sides to see if movement from the trains would tip them over. That did not happen.

"So that train theory went out the window," says Artuso.

However, one meter did go off. It kept flashing twelve times, then paused and flashed five times. This pattern repeated itself several times. Artuso said the flashing lights signified the date of the hotel fire: December fifth.

"That was pretty intense to have that happen," she says.

Katie's isn't the only well-known location Artuso and Gotham Paranormal have investigated. The team spent the night at the Tarrytown Music Hall in Westchester, New York. Theaters have a long history of paranormal activity, and Tarrytown is no exception, with unexplainable occurrences taking place throughout its one-hundred-and-thirty-five-year history. Lights mysteriously turn back on after closing, people hear an unknown singer performing vocal scales in the wings after hours, and talent refuses to stay in a particular dressing room because they sense a presence in there.

The team was setting up in the auditorium and talking with theater staff when they thought they saw someone coming down the aisle toward them. But, by the time everyone had turned around, the figure was gone – vanished in front of their eyes, she says.

Investigators also heard singing and humming in the dressing room, and a xylophone played by itself in the basement, says Artuso. As well, every digital recorder used that evening captured a steady whistling, like someone whistling a tune, throughout the entire investigation.

"But no one else was in there except us," she says.

"They had a worker who used to whistle while he worked. That's what he'd do. And he passed away four years before the investigation."

What's most memorable about the investigation for her is every claim theater staff made was backed up by the experiences the team had that night, which is rare, she says.

"We validated that they're not going crazy, because we heard it too," says Artuso.

What does a lifetime of encounters with the dead and spending long nights in dark buildings looking for spirits amount to? Artuso is convinced something is out there, but what it is, she doesn't know yet. And she says we might never know, at least as long as we're alive.

But she intends to keep looking for answers with the help of her husband and sons and dedicated team of investigators.

19 LYNDA QUIRINO

For more than forty years, Lynda Quirino has investigated ghosts and hauntings in her home and native land of Canada, often as a freelancer – meaning she'd venture into creaky old homes and abandoned buildings on her own, armed only with a flashlight and tape recorder.

"Which isn't something I'd recommend," she says, many years later.

Indeed, being a solo investigator, especially an inexperienced one, which Quirino was when she entered the business at eighteen years of age in her hometown of Montreal, Quebec, there are dangers to this pseudo profession, on both the physical and spiritual level.

For one, roaming around old buildings, often long since emptied and left to disrepair, can be dangerous. Weakened floorboards can collapse under the weight of a footstep, and whole walls have been known to come down without warning.

But there's also a risk, at least some people believe, to communicating with ghosts. Stories of investigators not protecting themselves and having a spirit follow them home, or even attach themselves to someone who is unprepared, do make the rounds. Of course there are those who fear demons and other negative entities are just lurking in the dark, waiting to pounce on someone.

What Quirino quickly discovered is the "risk" that came with sharing her passion for the paranormal with others. This was especially the case back when she started investigating in the 1970s, long before ghost-hunting shows were all the rage on television.

"People laughed at me at first," says Quirino. "Especially when you're eighteen years old, you're really interested in doing this, and people ask, 'What kind of hobbies do you have?' And I'd say, 'I investigate strange, odd, paranormal things' And they'd say, 'You're kidding me, right? Those things don't exist, right?'"

Teasing and laughing was generally the first response eighteen-year-old Quirino would get, but, once she was one on one with someone and the fear of ridicule had abated, she would get a different reaction from people – one of openness and honesty, she says.

"Okay, so I've got a problem...," people would say to her.

Quirino has found even the most skeptical of people have stories. And those people are willing to share, and even believe, as long as groups of people aren't around to hear them talk about it. Even the closest of friends would react this way.

Quirino's interest began with a personal experience when she was young, about three or four years old. The experience is tied in with her first memories, she says. The family had a summer cottage in the Laurentian Mountains, which is a vast mountain range in Southern Quebec. Quirino's grandfather was a construction worker who built the cottage himself.

The cottage was two stories – a main floor and a basement – and Quirino's parents would put her to sleep in her crib in the basement when she was little. She recalls seeing what she referred to as "funny faces" floating towards her out of the dark. She says they'd look at her, she'd look at them, then they'd float away.

She would see both men and women, but the men had these strange hats on, which she described to her mother as "bent," says Quirino. Her mother never ridiculed her when she brought this up. In fact, both were creative and open-minded people who often made the effort to ask their daughter about these weird experiences she was having.

One day, the family was watching "Dudley Do-Right", an animated series that was part of *The Rocky and Bullwinkle Show*, which depicted the humorous adventures of a Canadian Mountie. When Quirino saw the hat the hero was wearing, she stood up, pointed at it, and said that was the kind of hat she saw the men wearing in the cottage's basement.

"Oh, well, that's a Mountie's hat," her dad told her.

Years later, while talking with her grandfather about her nightly visitors in the cottage, he explained to her the basement existed before he built the cabin, and the previous structure was an old Mountie station, says Quirino.

Quirino continued to see spirits throughout her young life, until they simply stopped paying her visits when she was ten years old. Instead of relief, she was upset the ghosts, for whatever reason, didn't come to her. However, she maintains she still gets a feeling whenever spirits are present.

"I never stopped wanting to know more about them," she says. "And I loved it when people I knew had experiences that they told me about, because I realized I wasn't alone, and that's the number one thing. And of course it piqued my interest."

Quirino eventually married, and in 1986, her husband was transferred from Montreal to Toronto, in the neighbouring province of Ontario. Once the family was settled in, she decided to take up investigating again and joined

Toronto Ghosts and Hauntings Research Society. She remained a part of the team until 2003, when she opted to return to investigating on her own.

She continued to do so until 2012. By then the Quirinos had moved to Georgina, a smaller community outside Toronto. Having several years as a solo investigator under her belt and having built up a name for herself in the paranormal community, she found herself doing a lot of lectures on ghosts and hauntings at the local library.

Instead of drawing a small crowd of interested people, Quirino was surprised to have a hundred guests attend these lectures, many of whom wanted to hunt ghosts themselves. In the end, they talked her into starting a group of her own, and Georgina Paranormal Society was founded in 2012.

"People said to me, why don't you start one up here? We'd really like to be a part of it. So I did," she says.

Childhood encounters aside, Quirino considers one of her first solo investigations at a home in Hudson, Quebec, as one of her most profound paranormal experiences. She always focused on alleged residential hauntings and continues to do so. But back then, in a world with no internet, she relied on word of mouth to find investigations.

She heard about this case from a friend of hers while in prep-school. The friend told her about an old lady who lived in an old home and had objects being tossed about by someone unseen. Quirino agreed to help the woman and visited her, armed only with a notebook, flash camera, and tape recorder.

Thinking back, Quirino remembers meeting the lady,

who agreed to take Quirino on a tour of the home after they had a discussion about the case while enjoying a cup of tea... in one of the most active rooms in the house.

"Which was the living room. It had a gorgeous fireplace. All stone. It was beautiful," says Quirino.

Being a fledgling investigator, she took her line of questioning from the written work of veteran paranormal investigator and parapsychologist Lloyd Auerbach, who penned the seminal volume *ESP, Hauntings and Poltergeists*. Quirino asked the woman when she'd moved into the house, what experiences she had, etcetera. She deviated from her list of questions at one point and asked the homeowner if she really believed what was happening inside the house was real.

"Yes," the woman replied.

"So you really believe this? You don't think that they're a figment of your imagination?" Quirino continued.

"Absolutely not!"

"Gosh, I wish something would happen to prove that they're here."

Be careful what you wish for, Quirino says, as a moment later a huge, crystal ashtray flew off the fireplace mantel, whooshed past her ear, and hit the wall behind her with such force it dented the wall.

Quirino says that was a first to have something large fly across a room like that. And it left her feeling both frightened and intrigued. In the end, intrigue won over fear, and she asked to see the rest of the house.

"That's one of the most frightening and intriguing things that's ever happened to me," she says.

One would think seeing dead Mounties as a child and having an ashtray thrown at her would be the highlights of her career as a paranormal investigator. Quirino has had her fair share of visitations, moving objects, disembodied voices, and unseen things touching her during the last forty years.

But there was a case in Mount Albert, Ontario, in 1991 that stands out, she says. This occurred during her freelance days, but Quirino found herself joining a group of investigators who were called to a home in a suburban neighbourhood. The lady of the house claimed she was being pushed by an unseen spectre in the home, and most of these "attacks" occurred on the staircase.

Being more than thirty years ago, the team had the basics and set up an old video camera at the base of the stairs to capture whatever it could. Quirino says the team was there all night, and absolutely nothing happened... until it was time to pack up.

As soon as all the equipment was put away, at about 5:30 a.m., the temperature in the house suddenly dropped. This prompted Quirino and another investigator to look at the stairs, where they saw a woman appear.

"She was as solid as you or me," says Quirino. "She comes gliding down the stairs, but the weird part was she had no feet."

The footless woman blew past Quirino and the other investigator and out the front door, she says. The two investigators looked at each other and agreed not to say what they saw at that moment, but to write down the encounter in their notebooks. Then the other would read what they'd written. This would be the best way to figure out if they'd seen the same thing.

It turns out they had, she says.

Quirino still uses cameras — both digital and film — and digital recorders. She even brings an old-school tape recorder along with her as well as a Spirit Box. Like many experienced investigators, she prefers to use the basics and the equipment she used when she was starting out.

She used to bring an old transistor radio along on investigations and would tune in to the dead, static-filled air between stations. If spirits wanted to talk to her, they could probably communicate using that dead air, much like in the classic movie *Poltergeist*, she says.

To her surprise, she captured a fair share of EVPs that way for the better part of ten years.

"I had some success with it. I actually did."

And, as with many veterans in the field, she finds she's her own best piece of equipment, she says.

"I can ascertain what's going on. I walk in, and I know this place is active, and I know where to go," says Quirino. "Trust your instincts."

What do her instincts tell her about what's going on in the unseen world around us? She's convinced there's a level of existence just beyond ours that people can tap into if the circumstances are right, be it weather or frequency range on a radio, and talk to whoever is there.

"Some people, when they pass, they might hang on to being here for a period of time because they have things to settle," says Quirino. "I do think, for the most part, we can really tap into what's going on in a different world, in a different frequency."

Until a spirit taps someone on the shoulder and lays out everything that happens when we die, Quirino is convinced we're only going to catch a glimpse of what that other existence is. And she hopes anyone who decides to become an investigator does so for the right reasons – to find answers.

Which she will continue to do until she gets the answers she seeks.

20 ROBERT BRADLEY

Unlike many paranormal investigators, Robert Bradley didn't find his way into the profession because of a personal experience he had as a child. He became a paranormal investigator because of a gift from his wife.

Bradley, who is now a part of the Center for Paranormal Research and Investigation in Richmond, Virginia, was a fan of *Ghost Hunters*. His wife bought him a ticket to a weekend retreat with Jason Hawes and Grant Wilson at a haunted inn the duo own in Whitefield, New Hampshire, back in 2010.

"Thirty people got to go, and my wife got me a ticket," says Bradley. "I wanted to go up and meet them, doing the fanboy thing."

So Bradley flew up to Maine and rented a car to drive himself to the Spalding Inn. He says it didn't take long upon arrival for him to see things he couldn't explain. As the weekend progressed and the guests were led on tours of the historic property, Bradley became more and more convinced something was going on at the inn.

There was a room in particular, in the coach house, he remembers clearly. Bradley, another guest, and the guest's nine-year-old daughter turned the lights out, plunging the room into darkness save for what light spilled through the room's single window.

Just as Bradley was about to think the experience a bust, something walked between the trio and the window, he says.

The group jumped back with a start, says Bradley. The dad was searching in desperation for the light switch, and the daughter was slapping the walls near the window with the palms of her hands trying to find whoever... or whatever... walked across their view.

"All of a sudden, I'm very interested," says Bradley. A chemist by trade, he, like many scientists, needs to see hard evidence before becoming a believer.

Prior to that moment, Bradley had no real interest in the paranormal. He watched *Ghost Hunters* strictly because he enjoyed the interaction between the investigators and because the team didn't always find ghosts at the locations they investigated.

His interest was further cemented when he found out the extra night his wife had booked for him at the Spalding Inn was at a time when the inn was scheduled to be closed. With a blizzard raging outside, and no desire to trek out in it, he asked Jason Hawes what he should do – especially given his wife had paid for the extra night. Hawes told Bradley he was welcome to stay, even though no staff would be on duty.

The manager remained with Bradley for part of the time. They could hear furniture move about upstairs, even though no one else was present, he says.

"I ended up sleeping in the lobby with the TV on because I couldn't sleep in my room. It was so noisy above me, like someone was moving furniture and stuff," says Bradley.

By the next morning, Bradley was a believer. Or, at least, enough of a believer he wanted to learn more about the strange encounters he'd had at the Spalding Inn. He says Grant Wilson connected him with the Center for Paranormal Research and Investigation, as Wilson and Hawes were friends with the group's founders. The appeal for all involved was Bradley's scientific background and approach to investigations.

For Bradley, data is everything. But he's also had his share of excitement while trudging through allegedly haunted locations. And, when it comes to excitement, he counts Pennhurst Asylum in Spring City, Pennsylvania, among the most memorable.

A former mental institution, Pennhurst had a notorious reputation for being understaffed, dirty and violent, with several allegations of patient abuse that eventually led to it being closed in 1987. It's also got a reputation for being haunted, hosts the No. 1 haunted attraction in the United States every October, and welcomes paranormal investigators with open arms.

The Center for Paranormal Research and Investigation was invited to explore the property, so the team answered the call and conducted an overnight investigation. At one point, Bradley found himself standing in a third-floor hallway in a part of the asylum where the team had set up several environmental sensors.

He was setting up a recorder in hope of capturing some compelling audio when he heard what sounded like someone moving a table or chair down the hallway, out of eyesight. So Bradley went to investigate, and stopped at the stairwell to ask his teammates on the floor below if they heard anything too.

The other investigators joined him and found themselves staring down the hallway, where they still heard sounds, like someone moving furniture, says Bradley. The environmental sensors cast quite a bit of light, so Bradley stepped out of them into the dark.

And something ran toward him, arms outstretched almost like a zombie, from down the hall!

"It was a big, dark figure," he says. "And I fell. We'll leave it at that."

All of the team's environmental sensors went off as well, signalling something moved by them. But Bradley says the dark figure was nowhere to be seen.

Although he enjoys a good scare and an exciting adventure, Bradley still prefers to capture his data. And the best data he's ever recorded, even after multiple visits, is Bacon's Castle in Surry, Virginia.

Built in the 1600s, Bacon's Castle is the oldest brick structure in the state of Virginia. A historic landmark where, over the years, visitors have heard disembodied voices and seen fireballs and even floating heads move about the property. Many have been captured on audio and film.

Bradley and the Center for Paranormal Research and Investigation have visited the former plantation multiple times and are able to treat it like a laboratory, which is a crucial component for scientific research.

"We've got a really nice relationship with the people who run the place," says Bradley.

This relationship has allowed team members to conduct repeated experiments at Bacon's Castle, in a controlled environment, which has allowed Bradley to test theories over and over again. He's beginning to learn what many investigators call a residual haunting – past events replaying in the present given the right environmental circumstances – has nothing spiritual about it.

He says it doesn't matter if it's a disembodied voice or an apparition, the team has been able to reproduce the data enough that Bradley is convinced there's nothing paranormal going on at all.

"The data just screams that it's natural. It's a natural thing," says Bradley. "Now we're just trying to figure out what causes that."

The data can be found in a change in the area's geomagnetic field when these phenomena occur, and instead of cold spots, there is a spike in temperature by two to five degrees, he says. Humidity and barometric pressure is also increased almost every single time.

"It's a change in the environment, almost like it triggers something," says Bradley.

He points out this is what happens at Bacon's Castle. The team has reproduced the experiments at other locations, with slightly different outcomes. But he says the phenomenon is reproducible to the point where the scientist in him believes the experience is natural.

"As a scientist, this just screams that there's a natural cause for this."

Bacon's Castle also provides the team the opportunity to "dip their toes" into the world of interactive activity, the kind where doors open and shut on their own etcetera. Bradley says this is a completely different phenomenon and almost can't be reproduced, save for two things.

When a door opens or shuts on its own, someone gets touched, or some other form of interactive experience occurs, there's a spike in ionizing radiation that's two to three times greater than the background radiation, he says. And there's a more intense change in the geomagnetic field than the change that occurs in non-interactive activity.

All this makes Bacon's Castle an invaluable place to investigate and research the paranormal, says Bradley. The team visits the location twice a year, at different times of the day and night, to test the theories under different conditions.

"It's where we get the best data," he says. "It's really interesting to me, because I'm a data nerd. I've got to see the data. If it's just a personal experience, it means nothing. I've got to see that data."

Ever since he started investigating the paranormal, Bradley has sought out a place like Bacon's Castle, because he's wanted to apply the scientific method to the field. He believes this is crucial to understanding what is happening around us and what occurs when we die. And he feels fortunate to work with the Center for Paranormal Research and Investigation because the team is made up of current and former scientists and engineers.

A police officer and even a data analyst from NASA are among the ranks, says Bradley.

"We have a guy who's a professional electromagnetic engineer," he says. "We've brought these people in with all these skill sets."

The team doesn't go into Bacon's Castle, or any other location, with a bunch of flashy equipment like what's seen on many television shows, he says. All they look for and test are audio and visual phenomenon, which is the best to test and retest and validate. They also use Geiger counters and other scientific environmental equipment to correlate with the audio and visual data.

Although he doesn't count personal experiences as scientifically valid, Bradley has had his fair share of them, much like the encounter he had in that hallway at Pennhurst. A standout one occurred at another mental institution – St. Albans Sanatorium in Radford, Virginia. And sure enough, it's considered the most haunted location on America's east coast.

The hospital was once an all-boys Lutheran school notorious for bullying and unhealthy competition in the athletic department. As a result, several suicides were said to occur on campus. Once it became a sanatorium, St. Albans was the site of many experimental mental health treatments like electroshock therapy and lobotomies, and patients were killed as a result, or permanently disabled.

Suffice to say, there's a lot of paranormal activity reported on the property, and that brought Bradley and company to investigate.

Bradley stood atop what was called the grand staircase, with the majority of his teammates off on the right landing and hallway. The investigation hadn't started yet, he says. Everyone was just getting the lay of the land.

"And I looked off to my left, and there was a guy standing there," he says. "He was just looking at me, like I'm looking at you."

At first, Bradley thought this was a homeless person, as there was a problem with transients sleeping and staying on the property, he says. So he yelled at the guy and ran after him, hoping to confront him about trespassing.

"His eyes got real wide, and he ran down the hallway. I chased him down this hallway, and the rest of my team came up behind me," says Bradley.

"They could hear him running; then all of a sudden they couldn't anymore."

Bradley stopped and looked back at his team. The guy had disappeared right before their eyes!

He's had many personal experiences at Bacon's Castle as well, says Bradley. In fact, as soon as the team walks into the building, they hear someone moving around on the second floor, even though the place is empty. This happens every single time they investigate.

Given all his scientific and personal experience, does Bradley have a theory as to what's going on when it comes to the paranormal?

"If I knew, I'd tell ya, but then I'd have to kill ya," he says jokingly.

All kidding aside, the data Bradley and the team have collected, especially from Bacon's Castle, points toward an Einstein-Rosen bridge, or a wormhole. This is speculated to link different points in the space-time continuum. Many scientists theorize wormholes are merely projections of a fourth spatial dimension, which is comparable to how a two-dimensional being could experience only part of a three-dimensional object.

"You've got to think, if you open a door somewhere, and it's really humid inside this one room, but it's not humid in here, the humidity is going to change in both places," says Bradley.

He says there's still not enough data to support the Einstein-Rosen bridge theory yet, but the Center for Paranormal Research and Investigation will continue to explore this theory further.

This theory, in turn, isn't so far removed from the multiverse concepts discussed elsewhere in this book.

"Who knows, it may have a spiritual connection, but it may not," says Bradley. "I can't really say. But we are getting some interesting anomalies, and something out there is opening that door, and it's not me."

One thing is for sure, Bradley and the other members of the Center for Paranormal Research and Investigation are determined to find out, and they intend to do so using as much science and healthy skepticism as possible.

21 CHERYL COLLINS

When Cheryl Collins was eleven years old, she decided to play with her mom's Ouija board on her own.

Her mom had told her the board was just a "stupid game" that "didn't really work anyhow". but Collins had an interest in the paranormal and wanted to give it a try despite knowing that playing with Ouija on her own could be a bad idea.

She spent the whole day playing with the board, and sure enough, nothing strange happened. At dinner time, she was called downstairs to join the family for supper, so she let go of the planchette, got to her feet, and headed for the door.

"And the planchette flew across the room," says Collins.

That scared Collins but excited her at the same time. She says nothing else happened afterward that she could relate back to the board. Collins knows now it's important to "sign off" when using a Ouija board in order to prevent spirits from passing through and having paranormal activity escalate... at least according to Ouija lore.

Regardless, the experience fuelled her curiosity about the paranormal. It also happens it wasn't the only weird encounter she had with the supernatural, as she's seen and heard things since that she can't explain.

So Collins started researching on her own; reading books and watching documentaries. She became a fan of paranormal-themed television shows like *Ghost Hunters* and decided that's what she wanted to do with her life.

"I wanted to be able to help people, you know?" she says.

She and her husband live near Atlanta, Georgia. And eleven years ago Collins learned her husband had a friend with Roswell Georgia Paranormal. How'd she find out? She saw the friend and his paranormal team on television. She says she pretty much pleaded with her husband to arrange an introduction, which he did. Soon after, Collins was part of the team.

The years passed, and Collins took part in many investigations. She also worked her way up the team's ranks before joining Paranormal Detectives of Georgia, which she is now the case manager for.

Like any paranormal investigator, there's a case or two that really stand out for Collins. She has one in particular that resonates with her: an alleged haunting that morphed into a tale of possession, resulting in an impromptu exorcism. The story became the subject of a book and an episode of the documentary series *A Haunting*. It's known as "The Exorcism of Cindy Sauer".

Going in, Collins knew very little about the case other than the client was hearing things and experiencing unexplainable activity in her home. She was a self-described ghost hunter and, Collins later learned, had gone to an abandoned house where something allegedly got into her body, or so the story goes.

"This was a weird case. I always go in with an open mind, but at the same time, when I hear about a case, I'm skeptical too," says Collins. "The only thing I knew about it was it was possibly a negative case, and if anybody wanted to back out of a negative case, they could.

"I'd never experienced a negative case, so I decided I was going to do this."

In the paranormal field, it's common for investigators to refer to alleged demonic cases as negative.

Collins and two other investigators, Michele Lowe and Dan Bernstein, were to be the initial team members to meet with Sauer. Bernstein said he would meet them at the location, so Collins and Lowe decided to go for dinner and would meet Dan at the home.

While at dinner, Collins swore she heard her daughter call her name. She says she looked around the restaurant, but, obviously, her daughter wasn't there. She was taken aback by this, which Lowe noticed.

"What was that?" Lowe asked.

"I just heard my daughter call for me," Collins replied.

A look of surprise came over Lowe's face. "Oh my God! I heard my son call for me earlier this afternoon!" she said.

This set the tone for the entire evening, she says. When the team arrived at the "home", they discovered it was actually a double-wide trailer. For the record, on *A Haunting*, the filmmakers made it out to be a huge plantation house.

A boy came from across the street and told Collins and company the clients weren't home. Bernstein phoned Sauer and told them they'd arrived. She said she was on her way back to the trailer. Collins says Sauer arrived about ten minutes later.

By the time they got into the double-wide, Lowe was feeling uncomfortable. Collins sat down on a sofa and looked around the room while Bernstein spoke with Sauer. She remembers peering into Sauer's daughter's room and seeing a mattress on the floor and strange symbols drawn on the walls.

"Some of it was witchcraft stuff, and I was like 'This isn't good'," says Collins.

She let Bernstein know, as he was the lead investigator on the case. It was soon decided the team would start the night with an EVP session and see if they could get a feel for the situation.

The lights were turned off. Collins and Lowe sat on the love seat, Sauer and her daughter on a sofa with the family dog. Bernstein sat on the floor in front of them. Throughout the session, Bernstein looked at the floor, Lowe watched the recorder in her hand, and Collins focused on Sauer, she says.

"I wasn't taking my eyes off of her," Collins says.

As the EVP session progressed, Sauer began making weird gestures with her body, she says. Sauer twitched and jerked and rolled her eyes back into her head. At first, Collins took this as some lame attempt at theatrics.

"She started doing these weird things with her arms, like they were distorted or something. And then she started this growling stuff, and I was like 'Okay, seriously?'" says Collins.

She nudged Lowe, prompting her to look at Sauer. Lowe told Bernstein to look as well, so he turned on the lights. Collins says that was when Sauer's growling increased, and she went into some kind of "attack mode".

"Now, Cindy Sauer has these crystal blue eyes. She's a beautiful lady. And I knew it was real when I looked in her eyes and the blue in her eyes had gone. The pupil had taken over the blue in her eyes," says Collins.

"Just talking about it makes me shiver."

Then an unexplainable weird feeling came over Collins. All she knew was something was wrong in the house and with Sauer. She calls it a dark feeling, a fight-or-flight sensation.

Suddenly, Sauer "latched onto" Lowe, who is the team's psychic. Collins believes that happened because Lowe knew what was going on with Sauer, and she didn't like it. Collins says she thought Sauer was going to attack her.

Before that could happen, Sauer focused her attention on Bernstein, who immediately grabbed a copy of the Bible. He told Sauer he was going to count to three, and when he reached three, Cindy was going to come back, says Collins.

"She kept doing this roaring and growling and weird stuff, and Michele had her cross out and everything, and I was just standing there and watching everything," she says. "I didn't know what to do. I was two years into the team and had never experienced anything like that."

Bernstein reached three, and nothing happened. Sauer was unchanged. So he challenged again, saying he was going to count to five, and when he reached five, Cindy would come back to us, Collins says.

With Bible in hand, Bernstein counted to five. This time Sauer returned to her normal self, she says.

"She was sweating. She was crying. Michele was anointing her with oil and stuff. The blue just returned to her eyes," says Collins.

"That is the weirdest thing that I have ever experienced."

Collins doesn't recall any strange odours, like sulphur, surfacing during the encounter. Sulphur is often associated

218

with cases of a demonic presence and demonic possession. But this was almost a first for her, so she was very focused on what was happening between Sauer, Bernstein, and Lowe, she says.

She notes neither the daughter, nor the dog, reacted at all during Sauer's episode, which she finds strange. Typically, animals and children react to things that people can't see or feel. Collins says Lowe took a photo during the experience and captured the image of a shadow behind the sofa where Sauer and her daughter were sitting. However, the way the lighting was in the room, there shouldn't have been a shadow present.

The trio decided to call it a night after that and went for something to eat while they discussed what happened. Collins says she and Lowe were questioning themselves as to if the experience had even happened, and Lowe was contemplating quitting the team.

"But I knew that when I saw her eyes, that it was real," she says.

In the end, the investigation was turned over to another group of investigators within the team, and we'll continue the Cindy Sauer story in our next chapter with investigator Claudia Lee.

22   CLAUDIA LEE

When Claudia Lee became involved in the Cindy Sauer case, she was about a decade into her now twenty-year career as a paranormal investigator.

The co-founder of Paranormal Detectives of Georgia, she'd had encounters with high strangeness and conducted her own investigations long before the group came together. Her parents never discouraged her talking about the spooky things she saw and heard, chalking it all up to an overactive imagination.

"As far back as I can remember, I could see, periodically, off and on, full-bodied apparitions," says Lee. "And, for a while, we lived in a house that was pretty haunted."

This was in the late '60s and early '70s, and the house was built during prohibition, complete with a speakeasy bar in the basement with the brass railings of the era, she says. The activity was so frequent even Lee's mom got to talking about it. She worked for an engineering firm alongside the nephew of renowned psychic and paranormal investigator Sybil Leek, who was prominent in the 1960s. He offered to come and investigate the house, and that's when Lee learned there are people who investigate this sort of thing.

In the end, the investigation never took place. Lee's mother was afraid it would impose on the nephew, and didn't understand this was the opportunity investigators live for. The family eventually moved. Lee says it didn't matter where they lived, the family had experiences.

What brought everything to a crescendo in terms of Lee wanting to help others understand their paranormal experiences occurred when she moved to Atlanta, Georgia. She lived in a townhouse that wasn't particularly new or old, but it was situated near a reservoir and built not far from railway tracks – two things believed to attract spiritual activity.

According to some believers, water is a conduit for spiritual activity, and railways have a long and storied history of ghostly encounters.

Whether it was a result of the reservoir or railway, she would see or hear strange things on a daily basis, where she would normally have such an encounter once a year, Lee says. This started on the night she moved in, which wasn't long after the September 11 terrorist attack. What she witnessed appeared to be a firefighter holding something up by the back of the neck.

"I associated it with September 11 because this would be a high, emotional time for people that would maybe trigger people into having these experiences," she says.

Experiences like this became a nightly routine and got to the point where Lee thought she was losing her mind. Lee's grandmother had had a brain tumor, and she feared the same could be happening to her. So she made an appointment with her doctor, who ran her through every test imaginable. In the end, everything came back fine, so the doctor recommended Lee see a psychiatrist.

"I talked to the psychiatrist, and he says come back when you have a problem," she says.

Lee ruled out every medical reason for what she was experiencing, so she turned to a friend who had met a psychic and paranormal investigator. The psychic had previously been in the travel industry, but was laid off after 9/11. He turned out to be Chip Coffey.

Chip Coffey is a self-proclaimed psychic who has authored several books on the paranormal, including his memoir, *Growing Up Psychic*. He's also appeared on a variety of reality programs like *Paranormal State*, *Psychic Kids*, and *Kindred Spirits*.

"This was before anyone knew who he was," says Lee. "And you know, he was really great."

Coffey came to the house and managed to calm Lee down and explain to her she was probably more perceptive to the paranormal than most people, and as a result, spirits would pay more attention to her. He introduced Lee to other investigators, and over time, she became a full-fledged investigator.

"What brought me to this is me literally thinking I need help, and then thinking how can I help somebody else in this situation, when you think you're literally losing your mind and there's no one to turn to and no one you can talk to."

Most of what Lee and Paranormal Detectives of Georgia investigate are residential homes and can't be discussed due to confidentiality. The Cindy Sauer story has been well documented in a book by Sauer and the *A Haunting* documentary.

Lee was on the phone with Sauer for weeks before Cheryl Collins and her team were able to visit the house, as Paranormal Detectives of Georgia were swamped with cases. Lee says she counselled Sauer as best she could leading up to Collins and company going in. The investigation would be led by the group's co-founder, Dan Bernstein.

"I could tell, because of the calls I'd had with her [Sauer], that it would be kind of a dark case," says Lee.

She wasn't able to attend the initial investigation, which was documented in the previous chapter, because she was sick. Lee woke up the morning after the investigation with one call after the other from the investigators, who were disturbed by the night's events.

"They had a really bad, freaky vibe," she says. "There was just a reaction that it was bigger than we could handle, because it happened so quickly."

The decision was made to return two weeks later and continue the investigation. This time Lee would attend along with team member Michele Lowe and Father Darren, a colleague from the local Catholic church whom the team calls on for help from time to time. The plan was to counsel Sauer as best they could.

"He's helped us in the past, going into cases, especially where somebody has a strong religious belief," says Lee. "He's come in, prayed with them, blessed the house, and it brings them peace."

At the time, there was no intention of performing an exorcism, says Lee. The intention was for Father Darren to counsel Sauer, assess the situation, and perform a house blessing. And no effort was made to conduct medical or psychological exams on Sauer as a result. This is generally standard practice before efforts are made to convince the church an exorcism should be conducted.

"If I recall, I think she [Sauer] had talked to a physician, because that's typically something we ask," she says.

What Lee learned later was Lowe had contacted Father Darren, who had already gone to his bishop and, with the information Collins and her team had provided, was given permission to conduct an exorcism if need be, says Lee.

Lee and the team arrived and were greeted by Sauer's

boyfriend. Right away they began to hear a disturbance inside Sauer's double-wide.

"We knew right then this was not going to be easy. She's either having a psychotic episode or something is happening here," she says.

Father Darren went in first and Lee followed behind him and introduced herself to Sauer, who was seated on the sofa. A lamp appeared to have been thrown, and lay on the floor. No sooner had the team entered the room than Sauer sprang up on the back of the sofa and began moving sideways on all fours across the top of the sofa – almost like a crab.

At that point, Father Darren pulled out his crucifix, Bible and holy water, and began praying, says Lee.

To put things in context, Lee explains Sauer was previously married and her late husband committed suicide in the home. Sauer wasn't living there at the time, but, due to financial restrictions, she had to move back in, says Lee. The community and her husband's family blamed Sauer for the suicide, as she'd left him.

The home was in a sad state, she says. The floorboards were plywood; the carpet had all been pulled up and removed due to the bloodstains from the suicide. Bloodstains were also scattered about the master bedroom.

Sauer's children lived with her and appeared to be going through some emotional trauma as well, says Lee. Graffiti decorated the walls of one of the children's rooms.

"When I say graffiti, it was just dark. Let's just say that," she says. "Not something childlike."

When dealing with Sauer prior to going in, Lee says

Sauer would describe feeling not herself at times, with gaps in her memory from time to time. She believes Sauer suffered some form of emotional trauma from all she'd been through and where she was forced to live.

The whole time, Lee felt she was watching a movie play out in real life. She'd had her own paranormal experiences, yes, but she wasn't convinced Sauer was possessed. It felt like Sauer could also be having a psychotic episode.

Regardless, the team calmed Sauer down and sat her in a chair. Lee says Father Darren started the exorcism ritual and turned to her, grabbing a vial of holy water.

However, Father Darren mouthed to Lee that the vial wasn't actually holy water at all, just common tap water, she says.

"He turned around, and he put it on her, and she had absolutely no reaction," says Lee. "But she did not know it wasn't holy water."

The ritual continued, and Father Darren anointed Sauer with an actual dose of holy water. Lee says Sauer reacted violently to this. He also gave her a communion wafer. Sauer started choking and behaving strangely.

Lee remained skeptical and wasn't sure if she should be frightened or not, she says. As an investigator, it crossed her mind that Sauer could be faking the whole thing. But Lee couldn't get over the foreboding feeling she had, or the fact Sauer's normally blue eyes were pure black.

The minutes ticked away. The ritual continued. Lee isn't sure how much time passed before Sauer ended up on the floor, her boyfriend holding her to the ground. Father

Darren prayed over her. Then stopped. Lee says Sauer seemed fine, her black eyes back to blue.

Everyone went outside for a breath of air, and they brought Sauer with her. The entire mood had changed.

Had Sauer's eyes gone black due to pupil dilation because of some psychological trauma? Lee isn't sure. But they'd gone from blue to black and then back again.

"Every person that was on the team, that was there, witnessed it," she says.

When they'd first entered the home, Lee plugged her camcorder into the wall, wanting to capture everything that happened on video for review. Upon review, none of the exorcism was recorded. All the footage showed was static, Lee says.

"And we got nothing really on audio," she says, adding the investigators had their digital recorders recording the entire thing.

"It was very, very strange. And I know, in the moment, I was very, very fearful."

Reflecting on the whole experience, Lee sees patterns – perhaps coincidences – that make her pause. Leading up to the initial investigation, there seemed to be forces at work that tried to prevent the team from getting to the Sauer home. Lee got sick; two of her investigators thought they heard their children crying out for help, making them feel like they should turn back. Other team members became ill prior to the second visit as well.

"After that case, I went home. I was done with investigating. It took me two weeks at least before I started thinking about going back out," says Lee.

Sauer is doing great today, she says. She met with Father Darren privately a couple more times one on one and has since left her boyfriend and remarried. She's also moved.

With experiences like this behind her, what does Lee think the paranormal is? She flips back and forth between believing in spirits and thinking perhaps the paranormal has something to do with parallel universes.

What she does know, based on her own experiences, is there's something more out there, and it's related to what happens after we die, she says.

"I believe it's human spirit. Is there something else going on too? Maybe," says Lee.

ABOUT THE AUTHORS

Jason Hewlett is a journalist, broadcaster, and podcaster with a degree in filmmaking and film studies. A lifelong interest in the paranormal led him to join Vancouver Paranormal Society in 2017, where he was a lead investigator and society director until 2020, when he and colleague Peter Renn launched the Canadian Paranormal Foundation. In 2021 Jason became the manager of The Paranormal Network, a YouTube channel dedicated to high strangeness. He is the writer, director and co-creator of the award-winning paranormal reality series We Want to Believe, narrator for The UFO Show, and co-host of Hunting the Haunted, all of which are on The Paranormal Network. In 2020, Jason and Peter co-authored the bestselling book I Want to Believe: One Man's Journey into the Paranormal, which highlights Peter's career as a paranormal investigator.

Peter Renn has more than 27-years-experience as a paranormal investigator. Born in London, England, he's been fortunate to investigate documented locations all around the world, and specializes in negative (demonic) cases. He's also a documenting investigator for an exorcist in Washington state. Skeptical by nature, Peter looks for a logical explanation first, before jumping to paranormal conclusions. Peter is an executive producer and the lead investigator for We Want to Believe, and co-host of Hunting the Haunted, which are broadcast on The Paranormal Network YouTube channel. He was director of Vancouver Paranormal Society for a decade, but left in 2020 to launch the Canadian Paranormal Foundation with Jason Hewlett.

ALSO BY JASON HEWLETT &
PETER RENN

I Want to Believe: One Man's Journey Into
The Paranormal

Made in the USA
Coppell, TX
24 October 2021

64595637R00142